BOEING
MODEL 377
STRATOCRUISER

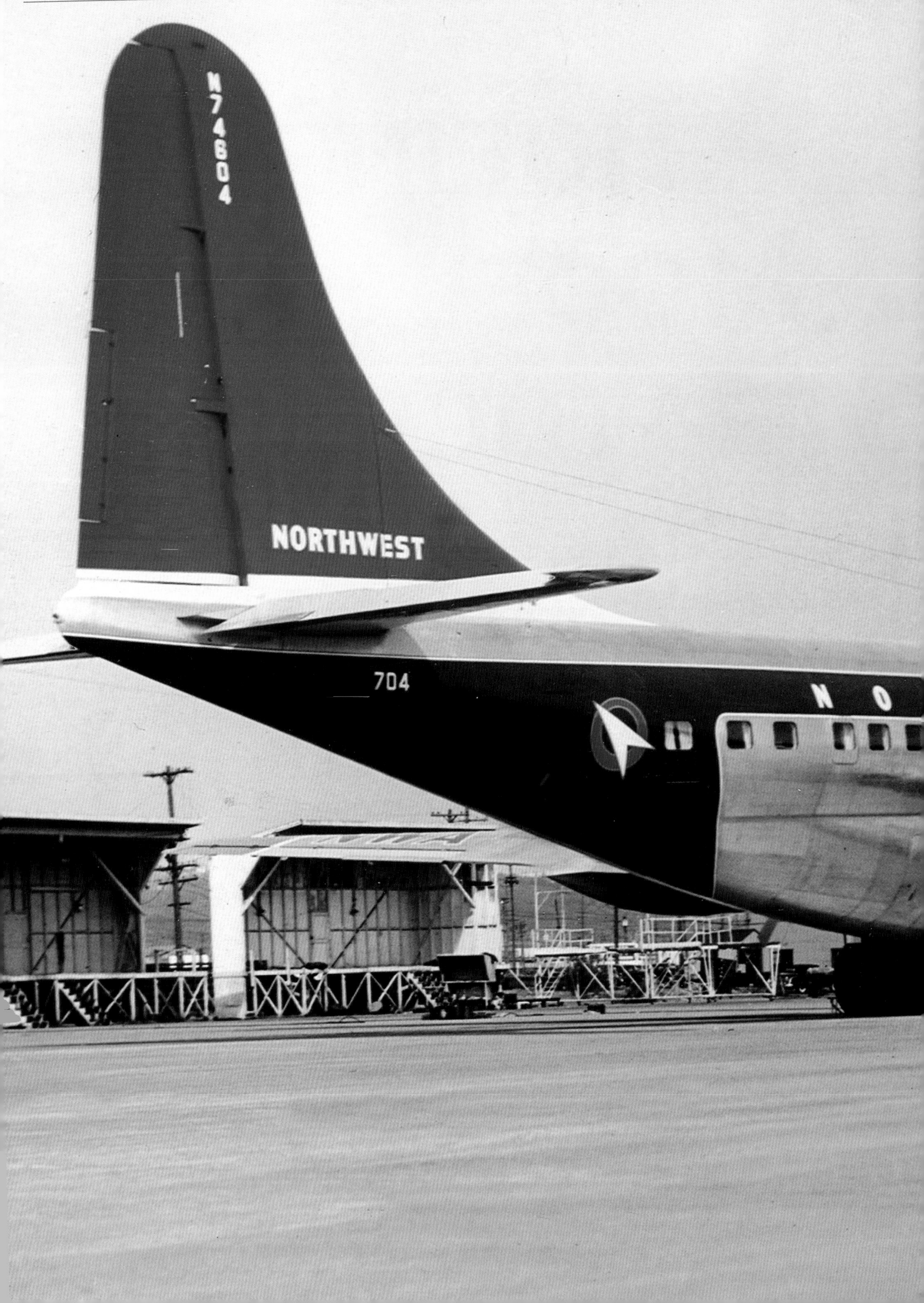
N74604
NORTHWEST
704
NO

BOEING MODEL 377 STRATOCRUISER

Robert Hewson

MBI Publishing Company

This edition first published in 2001 by MBI Publishing Company,
Galtier Plaza, Suite 200, 380 Jackson Street, St Paul, MN 55101-3885, USA.

Previously published by Airlife Publishing Ltd, Shrewsbury, England.

MBI Publishing Company books are also available at discounts in
bulk quantity for industrial or sales-promotional use. For details write to
Special Sales Manager at Motorbooks International Wholesalers & Distributors,
Galtier Plaza, Suite 200, 380 Jackson Street, St Paul, MN 55101-3885, USA.

Library of Congress Cataloging-in-Publication Data available

ISBN 0-7603-1197-8

Printed in China

PREVIOUS PAGE: Seen at the height of Stratocruiser production, during 1949, the
Boeing delivery line at Renton is replete with aircraft for Northwest Airlines, Pan
American and BOAC. The Stratocruiser in the foreground is the fourth Model
377-10-30 for Northwest, note the distinctive square windows. *Boeing*

BELOW: N90945, a Model 377-10-29, joined Pan American as *Clipper Monarch of*
Skies after PAA merged with American Overseas Airways. *Stephen Piercey/APL*

CONTENTS

INTRODUCTION

In aviation there is an era, that lasted for just a few short years after World War II, that has become steeped in magic. Those who remember it nod sagely and agree that we will never see its like again. Those who came later, yearn to have been there — to have lived with the sight and sound of the great piston-engined airliners that began to criss-cross the globe in the late 1940s and 1950s. Those were the days before the crushing science of revenue+passenger+kilometres times per-seat calculations directly affected operating costs — so absolutely crucial these days. The days before accountants ran airlines and there was no such thing as an airline 'industry'. The days before jets brought cramped and dehumanised air transport to the masses. The days when flying was still a most glamourous pursuit — and definately not for the likes of you and me.

In those days a succession of technical failures could turn a trip from New York to London into a three-day odyssey — and no-one thought it the least unusual. The days when you might not get there at all, if your sleek but always temperamental 'Clipper of the Skies' decided to throw an engine somewhere over the dark waters of the Atlantic. The days of cabin stewards and sleeping quarters, weather ships and Morse code. The days of the wonderful classic propliners.

Of all the aircraft associated with this golden age, Boeing's Stratocruiser stands apart. A true giant of the skies, the 'Strat' adopted the high technology of aircraft like the B-29 and B-50 and added some all-new features of its own. To many, the Model 377 is the definitive design of the great 'propliner' era of the 1950s. Though it had none of the sleekness of the Lockheed Constellation — nor the longevity of the great Douglas pistons — the Stratocruiser was the most statesmanlike of them all. Its portly, blunt-nosed exterior hid a cabin that was built for the utmost comfort, in an age when only the very rich could afford to fly. 'Strats' crossed the Atlantic and the Pacific in the livery of Pan American, American Overseas Airlines, BOAC, United and Northwest — the landmark airlines of their day.

Only 56 Stratocruisers were ever built, but they had an impact — and inspired a love — out of all proportion to their numbers. Experience with the Model 377 fed directly into Boeing's early jet airliner designs, aircraft that would all become world-beaters. The Stratocruiser pushed the technology of piston-engined aircraft to the limits, and sometimes beyond, as early technical hitches and crashes were endured and overcome. Even after the introduction of the jets there was no aircraft that could rival the Stratocruiser in terms of interior space and passenger comfort.

In another guise, the Stratocruiser had a quiet but important career as the US Air Force's C-97 transport and KC-97 air-to-air tanker. The KC-97 was the backbone of Strategic Air Command's tanker fleet for many years and KC-97s soldiered on in service for decades after the last airliners had been put to rest. The Model 377 design was also reborn in the family of Aero Spacelines Guppy conversions, fantastic outsize cargo aircraft that could haul chunks of the Saturn V moon rocket into the air and which ended their days flying Airbus wings and fuselages to their final assembly place in France.

RIGHT: Pan American's Clipper *Flying Eagle* cruises serenely over Windsor Castle on an early visit to Great Britain. Pan American established the first transatlantic Stratocruiser services in June 1949. *via Mike Stroud*

BELOW: NX90700 was the prototype Stratocruiser and made its maiden flight on 8 June 1947. Known as 'Number 11' (because it followed the 10th Model 367 Stratofreighter off the line), this aircraft was later delivered to PAA. *Boeing*

1 BACKGROUND AND EVOLUTION

In its first public statement on the Stratocruiser, released to the world on 15 November 1944, Boeing made some bold claims for what it described as 'the first of the great post-war super-transport designs with a prototype actually built.' The new aircraft would have a top speed of 400mph (644km/h) and would be capable of flying from New York to London non-stop. Boeing promised that the new aircraft would have the lowest direct operating costs of any land plane transport now built or designed, 1¢ per passenger mile or 5¢ per cargo ton mile, in the freighter version. The new aircraft was being designed and built by what was modestly described as 'the company with the greatest experience of any company in the four-engined airplane field. It has behind it the proven performance of the Boeing Flying Fortress, the Atlantic Clipper, the Stratoliner and the Superfortress.' The new aircraft would be the Model 377 Stratocruiser.

Stratocruisers have become synonymous with luxury air travel. The cocktail bar in the downstairs' lounge has become a legendary feature and the unprecedented level of space on board allowed the airlines to dream up all kinds of diversions for their passengers. At one stage Northwest Airlines hosted 'Strato Fashion Flights' on services from Chicago–

Minneapolis. At a cruising speed of 340mph (547kmh) the Stratocruiser would cut the travelling time between the world's major cities by a respectable margin. It could fly New York–London in about 11½ hours, New York–Tokyo in 22½ hours, San Francisco–Honolulu in 7¼ hours, New York–Stockholm in less than 12 hours and Miami–Buenos Aires in less than 13 hours. At the end of the 1940s there was one airline in the world that had such global ambitions, one airline that knew what the coming demand for air travel would be.

ABOVE: It is not difficult to see the influence of the Boeing B-29 in the Model 377 Stratocruiser. The airliner's 'double-bubble' fuselage was an extension of the B-29's while the wing and tail lay-out of both types was essentially the same. *Boeing*

BELOW LEFT: An early view of the prototype Model 377 over the Seattle shoreline during one of the first test flights. The flight test and development programme for the Stratocruiser would not prove to be an easy one. *Boeing*

BELOW: The story of the Stratocruiser is inextricably linked with its military sibling, the Model 367. Production of this aircraft far exceeded the Stratocruiser, and the C-97/KC-97 family also had a longer service life. This particular aircraft, KC-97G 53-3816, was the last of 888 C-97s to be built by Boeing. *Boeing*

ABOVE: The Sikorsky S-40 was the first of the Pan American 'Clippers', with the first aircraft (seen here in Mexico) christened *American Clipper*. The S-40 was the largest commercial aircraft of its day and the three that were built served exclusively with PAA, on the airline's Latin American routes. *PAA via William Doyle*

RIGHT: The immediate predecessor of the S-40 was the Sikorsky S-38, which joined the PAA fleet in 1928. Using a large fleet of S-38s Pan American and its associates built up an unparalleled network of services around the Caribbean and Central America. It was from this solid foundation that Pan American became the airline that encircled the globe. *PAA via William Doyle*

It was the airline that had done so much to establish long-range air travel in the pre-war years, the airline for which the Stratocruiser was designed and built — Pan American.

A CREATION OF PAN AMERICAN

The story of the design and development of the Stratocruiser is inextricably linked with that of Juan Trippe and the airline he founded — Pan American Airways (PAA). Trippe established Pan Am (as it was widely referred to later, but never then) in 1927, as the operating subsidiary of his Aviation Corporation of the Americas Inc. Trippe was a visionary and a master negotiator who managed to tie together the interests of three rival groups to establish his new company. He stayed at the helm of Pan American until a year before his death, in April 1981, and was renowned as one of the truly great figures of the airline industry and the history of aviation itself. During those decades Pan American became arguably the world's foremost airline and the company won a deserved reputation for trail-blazing and innovation. PAA was one of the great pioneers of long-range air travel, but operations began on a very modest scale — with a single Fairchild FC-2 floatplane flying a 90-mile (145km) mail route between Key West, in Florida, and Havana, Cuba.

Passenger flights were established between the same two points later that year, with an eight-seat Fokker F-VIIa/3m. By the end of the 1930s Pan American had quickly established a network of routes throughout Central and Southern America and its subsidiary airline PANAGRA launched passenger seaplane operations with Sikorsky S-38s in 1928. The Ford Trimotor became another type closely associated with PAA and, after the first example entered service in 1926, more of the type flew with Pan American than with any other airline. Flying boats remained the only true long-range airliners and Pan American graduated to the 22-seat Consolidated Commodore in 1930. The Commodores were the stepping stone to the first Pan American 'Clippers', the Sikorsky S-40. Trippe looked to the S-40 as a trans-ocean flying boat and therefore his solution to the quest for ever greater range.

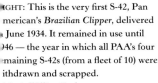

ABOVE: The Sikorsky S-42 opened up a whole new era for Pan American. It had the unprecedented capability of carrying a full load of 32 passengers over 750 miles (1,207km). In 1937 an S-42 flew as far south as Auckland, New Zealand, on route proving flights from San Francisco, while other S-42s conducted the transatlantic survey that same year.
PAA via William Doyle

RIGHT: This is the very first S-42, Pan American's *Brazilian Clipper*, delivered in June 1934. It remained in use until 1946 — the year in which all PAA's four remaining S-42s (from a fleet of 10) were withdrawn and scrapped.
PAA via William Doyle

In the early 1930s huge debates raged as to what was the best route to follow for truly long-range aircraft. The disciples of the airship were the leading contenders and great vessels like the *Graf Zeppelin* established the world's first trans-Atlantic air services. However, the fiery death of the *Graf Zeppelin*'s sister-ship, *Hindenburg*, in 1937 — and similar bad experiences elsewhere — ended the airship story almost overnight. In any case, airships were slow, difficult to handle and offered very limited lift capability. Land-based aircraft could still not offer the range of seaplanes, because suitable airports with long enough runways were simply unavailable — the United States had a handful and Europe had almost none. Aircraft designers were still arguing over whether their future airliners should be biplanes or monoplanes and most of the development work being done — almost exclusively in Europe — was devoted to large bombers for the military. It was military projects, born in a world edging closer to war, that gave birth to the Focke-Wulf Fw 200 Condor and the Farman 200. Both were pressed into commercial service (with the latter the more successful) but, as airliners, both were compromised by their bomber origins.

For the time being, at least, flying boats held the upper hand. They needed little in the way of facilities to operate — just a stretch of clear open water. While they could be difficult to load and unload in choppy conditions, this was generally a small price to pay. Unlike landplanes, they had few size and weight considerations. If a heavy flying boat needed a longer take-off distance to get airborne, then there were generally few concerns about running out of space. Most importantly of all,

flying boats offered the impression (at least) of safety on long trans-oceanic crossings. No-one claimed that air transport was yet a reliable means of transportation, with engine failures and other mechanical difficulties a routine fact of life. However, if a flying boat got into trouble it could simply land on the water below and await the arrival of assistance. This was a compelling argument — not least for the high-paying passengers.

TAKING THE FLYING BOAT TRAIL

Pan American embraced the flying boat ideal and, along with Britain's Imperial Airways and its great Empire-class flying boats, Juan Trippe's airline became the master of the art. The 38-seat Sikorsky S-40 which entered service in 1931 had all the appearance of a scaled-up Sikorsky S-38, but it was almost a brand-new aircraft. Weighing in at 17 tons (15.4mt) it was the largest commercial aircraft of its day and also the first to carry the 'Clipper' name for Pan Am (the three S-40s were named *American Clipper*, *Caribbean Clipper* and *Southern Clipper*). The S-40 was followed by the S-42, an aircraft that had a huge impact on air transport but is today almost forgotten. The four-engined S-42 entered service at the same time as the Douglas DC-3. It had none of the sleek, streamlined refinement that set the DC-3 apart — but the S-42 carried twice as many passengers, twice as far, just as fast. In fact, the S-42 began flying with Pan American in 1934 and so was really a contemporary of the DC-3's forerunner, the DC-2. The S-42s undertook a host of record-breaking long-range proving trials and PAA ultimately operated a fleet of ten aircraft, in a range of of different variants.

In 1935 Pan American showed, once and for all, that there was no real obstacle to regular trans-oceanic flying when it opened its first air routes to the Far East, flying from the USA to Manila, in the Philippines. The S-42s had paved the way, but Pan Am conquered the Pacific with the Martin M-130 flying boat — taking delivery of three aircraft between October 1935 and March 1936. The first flight from San Francisco lasted seven days, from 22-29 November 1935, and stopped at Honolulu, Midway Island, Wake Island, Guam and finally, Manila. The one-way fare from San Francisco–Manila was $799 — equivalent to about $15,000 in today's money. To those travelling on the route money was no object and at each stop along the way they were well looked after in a succession of fine hotels.

The Martin Clippers cut the travel time involved from many weeks to several days. Though capable of carrying up to 41 seats, most of the time the M-130s operated with very low loads indeed — often the crew outnumbered the passengers, and sometimes as few as one or two were on board. In reality, the M-130 could not accommodate more than eight passengers if it was to carry enough fuel for the critical San Francisco–Honolulu sector. The high cost of the tickets meant that the flights could still make money for Pan American — though the aircraft themselves also came with a hefty price tag ($417,000). This latter fact is tellingly reflected in the small size of PAA's fleet of Martin Clippers.

FROM MARTIN CLIPPER TO BOEING CLIPPER

Pan American Airways launched a new age in air travel with the Martin M-130, an aircraft that had been expressly designed to the airline's own specification. The S-42 had also been designed for PAA and, increasingly, this was how the airline dealt with the aviation industry. Trippe would issue a new (and demanding) specification, and the manufacturers would compete to meet it. The S-42 and the M-130 had actually been rivals for the same long-range flying-boat requirement — Trippe liked each design so much that he ordered both types!

With the Martin Clippers entering service in the Pacific, Pan American's engineers were already issuing their next set of specifications, this time for a large trans-Atlantic flying boat. The Atlantic was a tough nut to crack. Staging points in the Azores or at Foynes (near today's Shannon Airport, in Ireland) meant that the sector distances were comparable to those in the Pacific. What made the Atlantic so different was (and is) its long periods of bad weather and very severe headwinds, which particularly affect west-bound traffic. Because of these challenges, any new airliner would have to have very long legs.

In the end Boeing won the PAA Atlantic design competition and, in July 1936, Pan American signed a contract for six Model 314 flying boats. These aircraft outclassed anything that had come before them. They weighed 40tons (36.3mt), could carry up to 74 passengers and had twice the power of the great Martin M-130s. The first Model 314 was handed over in January 1939 — later than planned — and actually entered initial service on the Pacific routes. A number of bugs had to be ironed out before the aircraft was ready to start work on the

ABOVE: The Boeing Model 314 Clipper was the ultimate evolution of US commercial flying boat design. This aircraft, NC18607, was originally intended for Pan American but it was sold to the British Purchasing Commission in 1940. It then entered service with BOAC on that airline's war-time services. *Boeing*

RIGHT: Pan American's *Dixie Clipper* (NC18605) carried the first transatlantic passengers from the US to Europe. On 28 June 1939 this aircraft made its maiden voyage from New York to Marseilles and opened up a whole new era in air transport. The Clipper is seen here just prior to its delivery in April 1939. *Boeing*

Atlantic, but within a few months the Boeing Clipper was ready for duty.

The flying boat *Yankee Clipper* (NC18603, Pan American third Model 314) launched the world's first scheduled trans atlantic seaplane service on 20 May 1939. The aircraft flew from Port Washington to Marseilles, via the Azores and Lisbon in 29 hours. A mail service to Southampton began on 24 June The *Dixie Clipper* (NC18605) carried the first paying passenger to Europe on 28 June, with a return ticket costing $675 — about $12,500 today. In the eyes of many this new Pa

American service was little short of a miracle, and the provision of this regular reliable air link between Europe and the USA stood as one of the great technical achievements of the age. To PAA, with its wealth of transpacific and long-range flying experience, the Atlantic services were the product of solid operating procedure and proof of its fundamental competency. As a bridge between the Old and New Worlds however, the Clipper services stood for something more than that — something intangible but so very important. With the outbreak of war, in September 1939, the fledgling service was curtailed and by October it had been halted completely. Pan American's mighty Boeing Clippers continued to fly elsewhere in the world, and undertook many missions in support of the US military. While war raged across Europe — and soon the Pacific — Pan American's civil mission was put to one side, and the development of the modern airliner was interrupted.

As Hitler's war machine smashed across Europe the United States stood back and stayed out of a fight that it did not see as its own. The US did not enter the war for another two years, until the Japanese attack on Pearl Harbor (on 7 December 1941) shocked the nation into action at last. Until then, though their attention was diverted by the fighting in Europe, the US airlines and manufacturers pressed on with most of their plans. A whole new generation of large long-range landplanes was taking shape on the designer's drawing boards — aircraft like the Douglas DC-4 and Lockheed Constellation.

Pan American Airways had taken its first steps into the emerging world of modern airlines when it ordered 18 DC-2s in December 1933. Unusually, Pan American was not among the first wave of 'early adopters' for the DC-2 and the Boeing Model 247D, but it was not too far behind. Pan American's DC-2s were deployed on the routes of its associates, like PANAGRA in South America and the China National Aviation Corporation. In 1937 Pan American took on new aircraft in its own right when it accepted the first of what would eventually be a huge fleet of Douglas DC-3s. An initial order for eight was placed in October 1937 and these were split between Pan Am and PANAGRA.

ENTER THE STRATOLINER

1937 saw a most important event in the Pan American Airlines story — and, ultimately, in the story of the Stratocruiser. In February that year Pan American was finally granted landing and traffic rights in Britain. To serve on these new routes PAA ordered a brand new airliner from Boeing, the Model 307 Stratoliner. The four-engined Stratoliner was conceived as a high-flying long-range air transport that would, for the first time, be able to conduct landplane operations across the North Atlantic. Boeing had sowed the seeds of a whole new industry when it introduced the Model 247D, in 1933. However, the Douglas Aircraft Corporation trumped Boeing with the DC-2 and then the immortal DC-3 (the Douglas Sleeper Transport, as it was originally known). The DC-2 and the DC-3 were the aircraft that finally made real economic sense to the airlines, and boasted operating costs so low that they shook the entire transport industry. With the larger, pressurised Stratoliner

Boeing tried to open up a whole new market — reaching out fo comfortable, high-speed air travel at altitudes far above the ba weather. High-altitude, pressurised flight was still very much 'black art' at that time — just one man, TWA's famed Tomm Tomilson, was adjudged to have more flight hours above 30,000 (9,144m) than every other pilot in the world combined. Boein intended the Stratoliner to operate routinely at 14,000ft (4,267m an altitude that no other airliner could dream of reaching. Onc in service, the Stratoliner proved capable of operating comfortabl at 20,000ft (6,096m), and even higher. Boeing had the confidenc to tackle this ambitious goal because of all the work it ha expended on its Model 299 design — the aircraft that becam the illustrious B-17 Flying Fortress.

The Stratoliner was very much a product of its age — th post-Depression United States, all chromium with leather trim a place where anything was possible. The US was largel divorced from the storm clouds gathering over Europe and so in Seattle, the Boeing Airplane Company had time to spend o

ABOVE: NC19903 *Clipper Flying Cloud* was the last of three Stratoliners delivered to Pan American. It is also the only example that survives intact today – cared for by the National Air and Space Museum. The Stratoliner was the world's first pressurised airliner and was a stepping stone in the development of the Stratocruiser. In its own right, however, it was a disappointment. Only a handful were built and they did not live up to expectations. *Boeing*

RIGHT: Superficially the Stratoliner bore some resemblance to the Stratocruiser. It was powered by four Wright Cyclone GR-1820-G102 1,100-hp nine-cylinder engines, which were a far cry from the Stratocruiser's mighty 28-cylinder Pratt & Whitney's R-4360 Wasp Majors. This aircraft, the fourth Stratoliner, was operated by Howard Hughes as his 'flying penthouse'. *Boeing*

ABOVE: Pan American joined the Constellation club when it took delivery of its first Lockheed L-049 on 5 January 1946. Juan Trippe would have liked to have had his 'own' airliner, the Stratocruiser, in service by then — but it was just not available. By 1947 Pan American had began to introduce the improved L 749 Constellation (as seen here) on its North Atlantic services. *via William Doyle*

its new Model 300 airliner. All told, Boeing had very little airliner design experience with just the Model 247D and the Model 40-A of 1927 to look back on. The Model 300 was reworked into the final Model 307 design, a four-engined tail dragger that was a fatter, sleeker version of the B-17. The Stratoliner used the wings, tail surfaces and engines of the early-model B-17C. The lines of its 33-seat, pressurised fuselage were all-new though, and featured a characteristic upswept nose with a wide curve of flightdeck windows. The fuselage invariably had a polished all-metal finish and, despite its portly figure, the Model 307 looked like nothing else in the world.

The prototype made its maiden flight on 31 December 1938 — by which time Juan Trippe had already signed up for three. Another five aircraft were ordered by Transcontinental and Western Air (TWA), Pan American's biggest competitor in the US at the time.

The Stratoliner was the first ever pressurised four-engined airliner. This advanced technology — coupled with its promised performance — would be the key to its success, or so Boeing hoped. Another important Stratoliner innovation was its use of a new kind of high octane fuel that could maintain higher supercharger pressure, thus sustaining engine power at high altitudes. As interest grew in Boeing's new baby, and major European airlines such as KLM came to see it with serious intent, disaster struck. In March 1939 the prototype crashed into Mount Rainier, Washington state, killing all on board — including two representatives from KLM. This sad event, however, did not shake confidence in the aircraft. Though Douglas

had flown its rival DC-4E several months earlier in June 1938 and Lockheed had the bigger and better Constellation taking shape, nothing could yet rival the Stratoliner in terms of performance and passenger comfort — and the DC-4E was not pressurised. The Stratoliner could be configured in a 16-place Pullman sleeper layout, with no more passengers in reclining chairs. As a testament to its potential for luxury, one Stratoliner was bought by the billionaire Howard Hughes who used it as his own personal 'flying office' — this at a time when even small privately-owned aircraft were quite unusual.

THE STRATOLINER ENTERS SERVICE

The three Model S-307 Stratoliners (*Clipper Rainbow, Clipper Comet* and *Clipper Flying Cloud*) for Pan American Airways were delivered in 1940. TWA placed its aircraft into service first, on 8 July 1940. Flying a transcontinental service across the USA the Stratoliner could complete the journey in 13 hours and 40 minutes, two hours less than a DC-3. But as far as Pan American was concerned it soon became clear that the Stratoliner was not capable of doing the job it was designed for. Its payload/range capability fell well short of what was needed and, effectively, the Stratoliner could not cross the Atlantic and carry passengers at the same time. In fact it range was not even enough to undertake an adequate one-stop transcontinental route at home. PAA had plans to use its Model 307s on proving flights across the Atlantic, carrying mail, but this never happened. The PAA Stratoliners were redeployed to routes from the US to Mexico, Bermuda, the Caribbean and as far south as Brazil. Consequently, only nine Stratoliners were ever built.

Ironically, the Stratoliner did finally get the chance to fly the Atlantic, at the hands of the United States Army Air Force Air Transport Command. The PAA aircraft were pooled with TWA and handed over to military control once the US entered the

ABOVE: The Lockheed Constellation was the Stratocruiser's great rival, and its development was driven by Pan American's greatest competitor TWA. *Star of Ireland* (N86516) was an early L-049, which entered TWA service in February 1946. *via William Doyle*

ar in 1942. Repainted in olive drab the Stratoliner was given he service designation C-75. The C-75s were used to carry igh-priority VIPs, flew transport routes to the UK and South merica and were also used to train pilots for other four-ngined transport types. C-75s carried the likes of Generals George Marshall, Dwight Eisenhower and 'Hap' Arnold. The mall fleet of aircraft recorded 45,000 hours in the air, some ,000 oceanic crossings and 7,500,00 flight hours. Though they roved to be a disappointment in airline service, the Stratoliners ad a good wartime record and despite several close shaves, not ne was lost.

After the war PAA had its three Stratoliners returned, (the WA aircraft were handed back to Boeing). Very much in the wilight of their careers, the PAA aircraft still continued to rovide meaningful service. PAA figures for 1946 showed that ach of its Stratoliners spent around eight-and-a-half hours in he air every day. Flying from Miami to destinations like Havana, Nassau and Port-au-Prince, the Stratoliners carried 0,000 passengers in a year and, by the end of that year, they vere handling the 10¾-hour New York–Kansas City round trip very day. Ultimately though, the Stratoliner was destined to ecame a footnote in the Stratocruiser story.

By the time the C-75s were demobbed and returned to ommercial service the airlines were looking at a whole new eneration of airliners, driven by the technological advances of he wartime industry. Boeing was already putting the finishing ouches on its Model 377 Stratocruiser design for Pan

American, which drew heavily on the Model 345, better known as the B-29 Superfortress. A handful of Stratoliners did keep flying, with five aircraft going to French Indo-China in the hands of Aigle Azur. They survived into the mid-1960s and some were even active into the early-1970s. Today, just one example survives — a Stratoliner previously operated as the personal aircraft of Haiti's president, now owned by the Smithsonian.

COMPETITORS AND RIVALS

Though Pan American is most closely associated with the Stratocruiser, Juan Trippe made sure that his airline was also involved with Boeing's competitors and their alternative aircraft. In 1936 Trippe sat down alongside the 'Big Four' US domestic carriers and the Douglas Aircraft Company, and signed an agreement to fund the development of the four-engined DC-4E (not to be confused with the smaller, but successful, DC-4 that followed). In January 1940 TWA, with Howard Hughes at the helm, ordered 61 DC-4s, while Pan American ordered just three, two months later. Pan American specified a pressurised cabin (though no DC-4s were ever built that way) and by March 1942 PAA's order had grown to 28. The DC-4 first flew on 14 February 1942 but all available aircraft were immediately pressed into military service as C-54s (or R5Ds in the Navy).

ABOVE: The Model 377 followed hot on the heels of the military's Model 367. When the latter was revealed to the public in November 1944 its size and performance left most observers reeling. With such an aircraft already taking shape Boeing was well-positioned to provide the next generation of post-war airliners in the shape of the civilianised Model 377. *Boeing*

After the war Pan American went on to operate a staggering total of 92 DC-4s, which served mostly on domestic and Far Eastern routes. PAA was also an early customer for the Lockheed Constellation. This was a design that had been driven by Howard Hughes and TWA, but Juan Trippe had the good sense to see that it was an excellent aircraft and so PAA signed up for 22 Model 049 Constellations. Deliveries did not start until after the war, in January 1946. In June 1947 the more advanced Model 749 began to enter service with PAA and, when Pan American merged with American Overseas Airways, its Constellation fleet grew to 33.

The Constellation outclassed virtually every other airliner around and soon became such a dominant force in air transport that there were only two kinds of airline — those with 'Connies' and those without. Juan Trippe was frustrated that his great rival, the brilliant but manic Hughes, had made such a major step forward in aircraft design and, even though Pan American was a Constellation operator, Hughes had enough influence over Lockheed to dictate who was allowed to purchase aircraft, when they could have them, and who got the best customer support.

The Constellation would not go unchallenged — during the wartime years Trippe too had been busy. With Lockheed committed to Hughes and TWA, Trippe returned to Boeing — which had cemented faith in its mastery of large aircraft through the success of the B-17 and the B-29 bombers. As early as 1941 Trippe was already in serious negotiations with Boeing to develop a new long-range airliner that could take on the

Constellation and preserve Pan American's place at the top of the airline tree. What Pan American wanted was an aircraft that combined the technology of the Stratoliner with the performance of the Model 314 flying boat. With the Boeing Clippers, PAA had been operating large four-engined airliners a good ten years before any of its domestic rivals and the airline was keen to keep that advantage alive.

BIRTH OF THE STRATOCRUISER

By the end of 1940, Juan Trippe, A.A. Priester (Pan American Vice-President and Chief Engineer) and Franklin Gledhill (PAA's Vice-President, Procurement) had sat down and drawn up the specification for their new long-range airliner. They knew — literally and figuratively — that it would be the biggest thing in the airline's history. By January 1941 this demanding specification was being circulated around the major US manufacturers, and what it was asking for was extraordinary. Pan American Airways wanted its new airliner to be capable of carrying a 17,500lb (7,938kg) payload for 5,000 miles (8,047km) at 375mph (603km/h). It would be a landplane, without question, fully-pressurised and (probably) four-engined. It was up to the manufacturers to provide the best solution to PAA's needs, but before too much work could be undertaken World War II halted any thoughts of civil aircraft development.

During the war years Pan American maintained contact with all the companies it saw as prospective suppliers. The airline even entered into some tentative agreements with some manufacturers for a post-war airliner. In the end though, only Boeing could offer the (unbeatable) combination of availability, quick delivery, affordable price, necessary speed and desirable payload. The answer was provided by the Boeing Model 367, ordered by the USAAF in January 1942 as the XC-97.

ABOVE: N1039V was the second Stratocruiser to roll off the line and, even though it was part of the initial Pan American order, it was retained by Boeing for use in the Stratocruiser flight trials and certification programme. For these tasks it wore a colour scheme similar, but not identical, to NX90700. N1039V was handed over to Pan American in July 1949, nearly two years after its first flight. *via Mike Stroud*

Designed and built to a military specification the first XC-97 (the Model 367-1-1) made its maiden flight from Renton on 9 November 1944. It stayed in the air for two hours and five minutes. Two more test aircraft (both Model 367-1-2s) joined the flight trials programme. The XC-97 was conceived as a long-range military transport aircraft with a dual passenger/freight capability. None of the three aircraft saw any wartime service but on 11 January 1945 the prototype set a world record by covering the 3,323-mile (5,348km) distance from Seattle to Washington DC, in six hours and three minutes while carrying a 20,000lb (9,072kg) payload. This was not only faster than the Constellation, which a short time previously had set a coast-to-coast time of six hours 57 minutes, but also the P-51 Mustang which covered the same distance in six hours 39 minutes. Not only that, but the XC-97 was fully pressurised and could cruise at up to 30,000ft (9,144m) at a speed of 383mph (616km/h). Such an aircraft was virtually tailor-made for the Pan American requirement and both Boeing and the airline lost no time in talking to each other — albeit about an aircraft that a commercial customer could not (yet) buy. As early as November 1944 a name and model number for the new airliner

had already been adopted and announced by Boeing. It was to be the Model 377 Stratocruiser.

The appearance of the first XC-97 in public caused a stir because very little information had been released about the aircraft while in development. The existence of the DC-4, DC-6 and Constellation was all well-known and most observers had expected the DC-7 to be the first of the new larger American airliners to become available, but not until 1946. The new Boeing looked like being ready well before that. The XC-97's top speed was also a source of great surprise — indeed its record-breaking performance was most interesting for the insight it gave into the capabilities of the still-classified B-29. The 2 March 1945 edition of *The Aeroplane* noted succinctly that, 'even flying light, as the C-97 probably did, and at 30,000ft, the ground speed of 383mph was an amazing performance, and it must have shaken our constructors somewhat.' In the UK, airliner designers were still struggling with types such as the Avro York, a Lancaster derivative which was far outclassed by the new American designs. By early 1945 it was clear that the end of the war was not far away and speculation was growing about the new civil aircraft that would soon emerge. While Douglas and Lockheed had orders, Boeing had not announced any for the Model 377 — the discussions with Pan American went unreported. Boeing was not shy in promoting its new aircraft and made some weighty claims for it. According to the Company Chairman C.L. Egyvedt (the man who fathered the Flying Fortress), the Model 377 would offer 'the unprecedented low operating cost of one cent per passenger mile', when carrying between 70 and 100 passengers. *The Aeroplane* sceptically reflected, 'Well that sounds good, but frankly we'll believe it when we see it. Just at present it stretches the imagination a bit too far.'

At the end of hostilities, in 1945, Boeing emerged as the master large aircraft builder. It overcame immense technical difficulties to perfect the B-29 Superfortress, the aircraft which ultimately ended the war with the atomic bombs attacks on Hiroshima and Nagasaki. In the B-29 Boeing had proven all the engine and airframe technology that peacetime, and the new large airliners, required. With the end of the war the huge government contracts that had sustained mammoth production day and night across the nation ceased, and thousands of orders disappeared overnight. All the major manufacturers began to look to the civil market to take up their huge surplus in capacity — though they knew that the numbers would never match those of the wartime 'boom'.

Events proved to be particularly fortuitous for Boeing. Not only did the company start to work on commercial aircraft, but once the Cold War began in earnest Boeing supplied the huge fleet of jet bombers with which the newly-established US Air Force sought to equip itself. Then, with the outbreak of th[e] Korean War in 1950, the good old days were back in Seattl[e.] The armadas of B-29s and their B-50 siblings gave way to th[e] swept-wing jet-powered B-47 Stratobomber. This shiny ne[w] array of jet bombers demanded, in turn, an equivalent fleet [of] air-to-air tankers to support their global deployments an[d] operations. Boeing found itself in the enviable position of supplyin[g] not only the bombers but the tankers too. The modest total [of] C-97 Stratofreighter production soon ballooned with the arriv[al] of the KC-97 tanker variant and the best part of a 1,000 aircra[ft] were built. Boeing was lucky to have a ready-made design tha[t] could meet the renewed demand — but well before the war i[n] Korea that same aircraft was being readied for the airlines.

IMPROVING BOEING'S OFFER

The Model 367 was that aircraft, transformed into the Mod[el] 377 through the interest and intervention of Pan America[n] Airways. However, before the Stratofreighter (as the C-97 wa[s] known) could become the Stratocruiser, Boeing had to mak[e] some major changes. After a period of extended negotiation[s] PAA agreed on a downpayment of some $6 million — 25 percen[t] of the total contract — to help fund Stratocruiser developmen[t.] In fact, PAA handed over more than $7 million before i[t] received its first aircraft. In June 1944 Boeing returned to PA[A] with an outline commercial design. The new airliner woul[d] have four piston engines rated at 2,200hp (1,641kW), carr[y] 5,700US gal (21,577 litres) of fuel, have a take-off weight [of] around 120,000lb (54,432kg) and a cruising speed of 280mp[h]

BELOW: Apart from the Stratoliner, Boeing's only relevant experience with 'modern' airliner design was with the Model 247D. A credible and well-respected aircraft, it was eclipsed by the superlative Douglas DC-2/DC-3 and so it did not provide Boeing with a wealth of experience — or sales. *via William Doyle*

ABOVE: As the first Stratocruiser for Pan American, N1023V was christened with the illustrious name *Clipper America* (though it was soon renamed *Clipper Golden Gate*). The same name was applied to Pan American's first Constellation, and the airline's first Boeing 747. Ten years later, this particular aircraft was written off after a heavy landing at Manila, in June 1958. *John Stroud Collection/APL*

50 km/h). This was performance of which any manufacturer at the time would have been justifiably proud, but PAA wanted more. Trippe knew that basic aircraft performance would make or break PAA in the fight for traffic after the war. He asked Boeing for more speed, more fuel and higher operating weights — and suggested this could be achieved by using four of the new 3,500hp (2,611kW) engines that Pratt & Whitney had developed for the B-50 bomber. Boeing looked at the drawings once again and found that the new R-4360 engines would indeed fit on the Stratocruiser. By adding revised wing tanks an extra 1,200US gal (4,542 litres) of fuel could be squeezed into the airframe. All these changes pushed the (then unnamed) Stratocruiser's maximum take-off weight to 130,000lb (58,968kg).

THE DEFINITIVE STRATOCRUISER APPEARS

These changes were still not enough. Trippe again asked Boeing to go back to the drawing board and wring the maximum performance out of the design. Boeing found room for another 120US gal (454 litres) of fuel and released a further revised specification for the aircraft on 25 November 1944. Then by accident more than design — though all credit still goes to Boeing — the engineering department at Seattle became aware of new developments in superchargers taking shape at General Electric. It had always been planned to fit a mechanical turbosupercharger to the R-4360 engine, and this in itself was a very advanced feature. At its Schenectady plant, in New York state, General Electric had developed an entirely new turbo-supercharger that promised dramatic reductions in fuel burn.

GE already had some experience with turbosuperchargers fitted to Consolidated B-24s during World War II, and its refined design for Boeing promised to take operating economics to another level. On 4 January 1945 the turbosupercharging system was incorporated in the latest iteration of the Model 377 design.

Pan American had become the largest commercial contractor to the US Army Air Force during the war and this got the airline into a whole new business — the business of carrying freight. Before the war, air cargo had hardly existed and only mailbags featured as a regular load. With their experience of the China–Burma–India air bridge, the famed resupply operations by air over the 'hump' of the Himalayas, PAA's executives could see a whole new market opening up for the airline once the war was over. On 23 March 1945 the Model 377 specification changed again, this time to provide 910cu ft (25.7m³) of cargo space — up from the previous 675cu ft (19.11m³).

All the time Pan American was still asking for more. Boeing determined that fuel capacity could grow from 7,055US gal (26,706 litres) to 7,215US gal (27,312 litres), and that gross weight could rise another 5,000lb (2,268kg) to 135,000lb (61,236kg). Pan Am was not finished though, and when the final specification for the Boeing Model 377 was released on 28 November 1945 — just 87 days after VJ Day — another 400US gal (1,514 litres) of fuel had been fitted in outer wing tanks that had once never been considered.

The final Model 377 configuration that emerged was very different on the inside, but looked the same on the outside (apart from a 5ft/1.52m extension to the tail fin). All told, the payload had been increased by 10,000lb (4,536kg) while the maximum gross weight had grown by 15,000lb (6,804kg). Fuel capacity had risen by 2,000US gal (7,571 litres) and yet speed had also been increased from 280mph (451km/h) to 340mph (547km/h). This then was the aircraft that Juan Trippe and Pan American signed up for.

2 DESIGN AND DEVELOPMENT

When Boeing provided the first public details of the Model 377 Stratocruiser, on 15 November 1944, it claimed that the new airliner would have the highest overall performance of any transport built or designed. Top speed would be 400mph (643km/h). Its double deck ('double bubble') fuselage and large fuel capacity would provide unrivalled payload/range capability, carrying up to 100 passengers or 35,000lb (15,876kg) of cargo. Featuring an exclusive pressurised cabin the Stratocruiser would be able to maintain a comfortable cabin altitude of 8,000ft (2,438m) when flying at 30,000ft (9,144m). The Model 377 would inherit the unequalled aerodynamic

efficiency of the great Boeing Superfortress, and provide combination of high performance and very low operating costs

The Boeing Model 377 Stratocruiser was a direct descendant of the Boeing Model 345 (B-29 Superfortress). Its immediate ancestor was the Model 367, the Stratofreighter, which first flew on 9 November 1944. The Model 377 and 367 were constructed on the same production line at Renton, and the prototype Stratocruiser was built in sequence, slotted in after the tenth Model 367 (a YC-97 development aircraft). The Model 367 and Model 377 took the lower section of the B-29 fuselage and enlarged it to a distinctive 'double bubble' form

ABOVE: The most obvious difference between the Stratocruiser and the military Stratofreighter was the latter's cargo doors and cargo-handling equipment. This C-97 is seen tucking away its hydraulically-operated rear loading ramp, through the underslung clamshell doors that led to the main cabin. Boeing did consider building a commercial freighter version of the Stratocruiser, but these plans were soon abandoned. *Boeing*

LEFT: The prototype Stratocruiser thunders off the runway at Renton at the beginning of another test flight. Boeing styled the Stratocruiser as 'the first of the giant airliners to go into service'. While on the outside it was not significantly bigger than its contemporaries, the unprecedented internal volume that it offered set the Model 377 in a class apart. *Boeing via the Aviation Picture Library*

that in cross-section the fuselage had a figure-of-eight shape. he lower section of the bubble housed cargo and baggage but so provided space for the Stratocruiser's famed lower lounge. he main cabin was formed from the new upper lobe, which ad a diameter of 11ft (3.3m). To link the upper and lower abins, Boeing introduced what would become the ratocruiser's most talked-about feature — the spiral staircase, side an aircraft!

At the time the Model 377 seemed excessively large and was kened to both a flying ocean liner and a flying whale. It was so hard to believe that its blunt-nosed shape could fly so fast.

The XC-97 was powered by four 2,200hp Wright R-3350-23 piston engines — the powerplants that had originally been intended for the Model 377. However, Juan Trippe insisted that the mighty 28-cylinder Pratt & Whitney R-4360 Wasp Major be fitted instead (these were later also added to the YC-97A and all subsequent members of the C-97 family). In fact, the Model 377 proved to be quite similar to the USAF's YC-97B, a one-off VIP conversion that lacked the spartan cargo interior and clamshell loading doors of other Stratofreighters. The Model 377 used Boeing's 75-ST alloy structure and had a door and window arrangement similar to that of the YC-97B.

Depending on the seating arrangement the Stratocruiser could carry between 55 and 100 passengers, but none of its original operators ever used their aircraft at maximum seating capacity. A typical load was in the region of 60 passengers, in a luxuriously appointed cabin. In the sleeper configuration, so popular at that time, a Stratocruiser typically had 28 upper and lower berths, with another five reclining seats. At the end of the spiral stair-case was the lower cabin, which could accommodate another 14 passengers — but this space was often devoted to a cocktail bar with some lounge seating. But however it was laid out, the entire area was treated as free space for passengers and was never ticketed or sold.

The stairs were situated just behind the trailing edge of the wing, with the so-called 'observation lounge' stretching aft from there to the point where the rear fuselage began to slope upwards, towards the tail. Special cloakrooms were provided for male (forward) and female (aft) passengers and the Stratocruiser's underfloor galley arrangements (located forward) were the largest and best equipped of any contemporary airliner.

To speed up the flight test programme Boeing commandeered two production aircraft originally destined for Pan American. These were N1023V and N1039V, which were registered as NX1023V and NX1039V for trials flying. N1039V flew first, on 28 September 1947, followed by NX1023V on 17 April 1948.

ABOVE: Stratocruiser NX1039V, a production-standard aircraft, shouldered the flight test burden with the single prototype. Boeing suffered a range of snags and difficulties that delayed the Stratocruiser's service entry by nearly two years. This particular aircraft later suffered the sad fate of becoming the first Stratocruiser to crash while in regular service, with Pan American, in April 1952. *Boeing via APL*

Both aircraft played a major part in the mandatory Function and Reliability testing requirement. For this particular phase of the certification programme the Stratocruiser had to undertake sustained 200-hr flight schedule and make 54 transcontinental flights, replicating standard airline operations.

STRATOCRUISER VARIANTS
Although all the Stratocruisers that were delivered to the six primary customer airliners were structurally identical, they had some detail differences. The most noticeable of these were the 'Douglas style' rectangular windows adopted by Northwest Airlines and United. Stratocruiser deliveries ran from February 1949 to March 1950 and the list price of a new aircraft at the time was approximately $1,500,000 each.

MODEL 377-10-19
The Model 377-10-19 was the first commercial version of the Stratofreighter, dubbed the Stratocruiser. The single prototype Model 377 Stratocruiser (NX90700) followed the tenth Model

67 Stratofreighter off the production line — so it was referred o by all at Boeing as 'Number 11'. NX90700 was also known s the 'dog ship' — in the way of most prototypes — because it vas used to test a host of trials and development fits, and a ariety of on-board equipment. The -19 made its maiden flight n 8 July 1947 and was a Boeing-owned aircraft. However, it vas later bought by Pan Am and brought up to that airline's 26 model standard.

MODEL 377-10-26

Pan American Airways was the launch customer for the tratocruiser and bought the lion's share of Boeing's Model 377 roduction. Of the 56 aircraft built, 20 went straight to Pan American — Boeing gave these aircraft the model designation 26. When PAA took over the -29 aircraft that were previously perated by American Overseas Airways, they were modified to 26 standard. One Pan American aircraft, NX1039V (later J1039V), initially flew in Boeing house livery and was used for he certification flight testing alongside the -19 prototype which later also went to PAA). Pan American's Stratocruisers vere typically configured with 61 seats, though the maximum coach' layout was 81 to 86 seats. In sleeper configuration they arried 25 seats when 18 berths were made up to sleep 27 assengers. Pan American ultimately had a fleet of 29

Stratocruisers. All of these were subsequently upgraded with revised with turbosuperchargers that provided an additional 50hp (37.3kW) of power per engine.

MODEL 377-10-26 'SUPER STRATOCRUISER'

Ten of Pan American's -26 Stratocruisers were modified to so-called 'Super Stratocruiser' standard. These aircraft were all operated by the airline's Atlantic Division and were intended to provide extra range for transatlantic crossings. Extra fuel tanks carrying an additional 450US gal/1,703 litres of fuel (total load then 8,240US gal/31,191 litres) were fitted to these aircraft, all of which carried 'Super Stratocruiser' titles on their fins.

MODEL 377-10-28

SILA (Svensk Interkontinental Luftrafik) was a predecessor of today's SAS (Scandinavian Airline Systems), a joint airline with Swedish, Norwegian and Danish ownership. SILA ordered four -28 Stratocruisers, for which registrations were allocated, but these were never taken up as the order was cancelled. The

ABOVE: Northwest Airline's Model 377-10-30s were the only Stratocruisers to be built with square windows on both decks. This plane wears the 'Orient' titles added to Northwest's aircraft some years after their introduction, when the airline restyled itself as Northwest Orient to reflect its links with the Far East. *via Walter Klein*

quartet of aircraft was acquired instead by BOAC (and later sold on to Transocean airlines). These -28's were configured with a private stateroom, situated aft of the main cabin, and had a luxury main cabin fitted with 55 seats. Each aircraft was different to its sisterships. In sleeper layout, seating fell to just 20 — with another 17 berths available to sleep 26 passengers.

MODEL 377-10-29

American Overseas Airlines ordered eight Model -29 Stratocruisers, with the first example delivered in June 1949. When Pan Am and AOA merged in 1950 these aircraft were all transferred to the PAA fleet. The -29 configuration was very similar to Pan American's own -26s. They were typically fitted with 60 seats and had a maximum seating capacity of 86. In sleeper configuration they carried 25 seats plus 30 berths made up to sleep 45 passengers.

MODEL 377-10-30

Ten Model -30 Stratocruisers were built for Northwest Airline (later Northwest Orient) and the first was delivered in Jul 1949. The -30s were notable for rectangular cabin window (earlier aircraft all had circular windows) and later in their live the Airline added a weather radar in a pimple radome on th nose — much like that fitted to the C-97A. The -30s were buil with a single 'luxury' layout in mind, seating just 61 on th main deck — or 28 when 16 berths were made up to sleep 2 passengers. Beginning in 1953 however, the Northwest 'Strat were modified to carry up to 83 seats.

MODEL 377-10-32

After Pan American, the British Overseas Airways Corporatio (BOAC) became the most important Stratocruiser operato

RIGHT: G-AKGH was the first of BOAC's Model 377-10-32s, six of which were built specifically for the British airline. Unlike the four ex-SILA aircraft that preceded them into service, the -32s had square lower deck windows — and a ver different cabin layout. *Boeing*

ABOVE: The first BOAC Stratocruisers, which began to arrive in October 1949, were the four Model 377-10-28s originally ordered by SILA. The Boeing press release that accompanied this photograph, of the third BOAC Stratocruiser (G-ALSC), described it as 'Seventy-one tons of comfort.' *Boeing*

with 17 aircraft eventually wearing BOAC colours. An initial batch of six -32 aircraft was ordered from Boeing, with the first example delivered in November 1949. The main deck of the -32 provided seats for 60 passengers, with 20 seats available when 17 berths were made up to sleep 26. In the BOAC aircraft

the lower lounge could accommodate 12 people — two less than most other 'Strats'. BOAC's fleet also included the ex-SILA aircraft and, later, the former United Stratocruisers.

MODEL 377-10-34

United Air Lines ordered seven -34s which, like the -30 aircraft, were all fitted with rectangular cabin windows. The first -34 was handed over by Boeing in September 1949. UAL was unusual among Stratocruiser operators in that all its aircraft spent most of their time on domestic services within the

ABOVE: All of United Model 377-10-34 Stratocruisers were christened 'Mainliners' and they served on the airline's trans-Pacific services from Los Angeles and San Francisco to Hawaii. After a relatively short service career the six surviving aircraft were sold to BOAC in 1954. *Boeing*

United States — though they did venture as far as Honolulu. UAL's aircraft were fitted out with a first class cabin for just 56 seats, or 20 when 17 berths were made up for 26 sleepers.

MODEL 377 HIGH DENSITY MODIFICATION

Transocean Airlines purchased 14 Model 377s from BOAC, the first batch of four aircraft (N401Q, N402Q, N403Q and N404Q) were fitted with a high-density cabin capable of carrying 112 passengers, in single-class seating. Four of the second batch of six aircraft, delivered in early 1959 (N405Q,

N406Q, N409Q and N410Q) were also refitted with additior seats — though not to the same 'super capacity'. They each h an additional 12 seats added and so could carry between 75 98 passengers in a two-class arrangement — depending on th original configuration. Later in 1959 Transocean took delive of a third batch of four aircraft. These were all former-UA Stratocruisers that had been acquired by BOAC and so were a slightly different seating configuration, however these aircra never entered TAL service as the airline went bust in 1960.

BELOW: The five aircraft that entered Israeli military service stand out as the mo unusual, and the longest-lived, of all the Stratocruisers. Israel implemented a maj modification programme that converted the aircraft into specialist transports for t IDF/AF. This example was the one-time N1030V, a former Pan American aircra which was converted into a swing-tail freighter, with a side cargo door. *Walter Kle*

ABOVE: The newly-added rear fuselage hinges, and the fairing for the tail opening mechanism (extending from the fin root) can clearly be seen in this view of 4X-FPW, along with sistership 4X-FPY which received 'C-97-style' clamshell doors as part of its, less extensive, cargo conversion. *Walter Klein*

STRATOCRUISER CARGO CONVERSIONS

When RANSA (Rutas Aereas Nacionales SA) of Venezuela bought its fleet of surplus Stratocruisers the airline began to convert them into freighters by adding a side cargo door (in the same style as the C-97). Two RANSA aircraft — YV-C-ERH and YV-C-ERI — were fitted with doors measuring 76in x 80in (193cm x 203.2cm). A third RANSA aircraft, YV-C-ERJ, was fitted with a much larger door that measured 72in x 142in (182.8cm x 360.6cm). A fourth aircraft, YV-C-ERK, was about to undergo its freighter conversion when the airline went out of business in 1966.

IAI 'ANAK' CONVERSIONS

Five Stratocruisers acquired by the Israel Defence Air Force

were also converted to serve as freighters. In IDF/AF service they were given the local name 'Anak', meaning 'giant'. At the hands of IAI all five aircraft were fitted with forward cargo doors. Three of the Stratocruisers — 4X-FOD (later 4X-FPZ), 4X-FOG (later 4X-FPX) and 4X-FOI (later 4X-FPY) — were then given underfuselage clamshell freight doors, just like those found on the C-97. These aircraft could carry 110 paratroops, 135 infantry soldiers or 35,000lb (15,876kg) of cargo. They were also fitted with an internal cargo hoist and a rear loading ramp, allowing small vehicles to be driven up inside the aircraft.

The other two Stratocruisers — 4X-FOH (later 4X-FPV) and 4X-FOF (later 4X-FPW) — underwent a dramatic swing-tail conversion. The entire fuselage and fin, aft of the wing, was hinged and could be folded 92° across to the right — allowing the aircraft to accommodate wide and bulky loads. The swing door was opened by a hydraulic actuator mounted in a fairing forward of the main fin and it was held in place by 12 latches around the circumference of the aircraft.

To give them some of the tactical operational capabilities of the C-130s the IDF/AF Stratocruisers were fitted with three braking parachutes (one large, two small) and provision for 22 RATO (Rocket-Assisted Take-Off) bottles on the aft fuselage sides. These dramatic modifications would have allowed the Stratocruisers to land and take-off from short unprepared strips in time of war, or for special missions. Once the C-130 became available for export to Israel there was no need to sustain the expensive-to-operate Stratocruisers any longer. The last aircraft were retired in the mid-1970s, though several ex-USAF C-97s did remain in Israeli service for several years after that.

BOEING MODEL 367
C-97 STRATOFREIGHTER, KC-97

The story of the Stratocruiser would not be complete without a brief record of its immediate predecessor, the Boeing Model 367. In fact, development of the two was intertwined, with both military and civil requirements expressed in the basic design. If the outbreak of World War II had not scaled back the ambitions and importance of the civil air transport industry it is quite possible that the Stratocruiser would have appeared before the Stratofreighter and, without the war in the Pacific, perhaps the latter might not have existed at all.

With America embroiled in a transpacifc war, the Stratofreighter was conceived as a transpacific military freighter

ABOVE: wearing its 'Pacific Division' credentials proudly on its fin, this US Air Force Military Air Transport Service Stratofreighter is pictured passing over Mare Island, in San Francisco Bay, *en route* to its first stopping off point in Hawaii. The C-97 was conceived as a long-range transport for the war against Japan and, as such, it was almost identical to Pan American's requirement for a new long-range airliner to serve its trans-oceanic routes. Described as a 'C-97 leviathan' by USAF public affairs copywriters, this Stratofreighter is actually the fourth (of six) YC-97 — part of an overall batch of ten pre-service test aircraft ordered in July 1945. *USAF via Walter Klein*

BELOW: The KC-97G was the last production variant of the C-97 family and an impressive total of 592 were built before the advent of the KC-135, in 1956. Beginning in 1964 aircraft attached to the Air National Guard were modified to KC-97L standard through the addition of J47 turbojets, to improve their overall performance. KC-97Ls soldiered on well into the 1970s with the ANG — this aircraft is seen in July 1973 with 'four turning and two burning'. *Stephen Piercey/Aviation Picture Library*

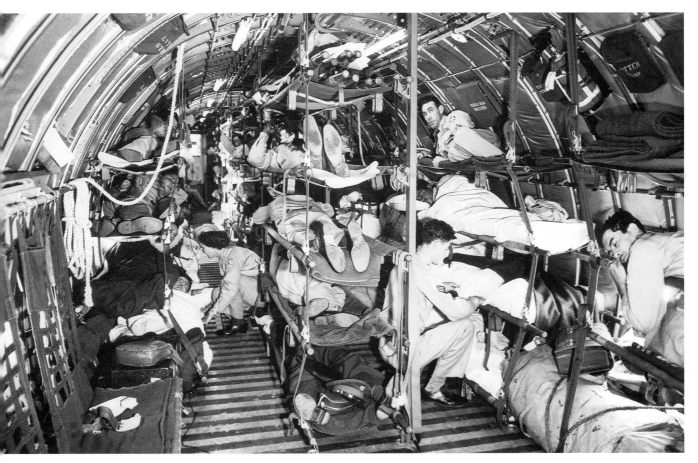

ABOVE AND BELOW: Unsurprisingly there was a stark difference between the interiors of the USAF's Model 367s and airlines' Model 377s. This C-97 (above) is rigged for air evacuation duties and is carrying casualties home from the Korean War. The C-97's pressurised cabin made it well-suited to carrying sick or wounded personnel, while its high cruising altitude made for a more comfortable ride. The passengers in this Pan American Stratocruiser (below) are having a more luxurious flight. Instead of stretchers, sleeping berths can be lowered from the cabin roof, while the de luxe seats could be reclined or even made up into double beds. *Boeing*

one that could carry heavy equipment at high-speeds over long distances. When the first proposals were drawn up for such an aircraft in 1942, it was the largest, heaviest, fastest cargo aircraft ever built. This was exactly the kind of aircraft that Juan Trippe was also looking for, albeit to carry passengers not war material. Typical loads were to include 155mm field guns, 2.5 ton trucks, or substantial numbers of troops. The Model 367 drew heavily on Boeing's Model 345 (B-29) design

ABOVE: Seen during final assembly on the production line, this is the first YC-97 the USAF. Ten pre-production YC-97s were built before the prototype Model 37 Stratocruiser followed them into the daylight. The YC-97s were a great success, a when the Cold War followed the Korean War in ernest, Boeing was assured of a ready market for its military aircraft. *Boeing*

BELOW: The first YC-97A made its maiden flight on 28 January 1948, to join wha Boeing described as 'the first team of the air.' The YC-97A shared many of the basic features of the Model 377, such as its 75ST alloy structure, R-4360 engines, enlarged (and folding) tail and boosted rudder controls. *Boeing*

ABOVE: Within months of the maiden flight of the first YC-97A the type had proven itself in the Berlin airlift — the third aircraft was dispatched to Germany for some real service experience. Once the USAF took the decision to acquire production-standard C-97As, the YC-97s remained in service. They were upgraded to an equivalent level, gaining the chin radome fitted to the C-97As. This YC-97A is seen over San Francisco's Golden Gate Bridge. *USAF via Walter Klein*

BELOW: The two turboprop powered YC-97J testbeds may be only a footnote in the C-97 story, but they hold a place of their own in the overall saga of the Stratocruiser. The YC-97Js were built to test the Pratt & Whitney T-34 turboprop engine, and a new three-bladed prop. They set many in-service performance records but the new engines were not adopted. However, both aircraft were later used to produce the B377SG Super Guppy conversion. *USAF via Walter Klein*

experience, and the basic design was built up from the proven
B-29 wing mated to an enlarged B-29 main fuselage.

When the first XC-97 (Model 367-1-1) made its maiden
flight on 9 November 1944 it was powered by four Wright
R-3350 piston engines, and these were fitted to all three XC-97
prototypes. In July 1945 the USAAF (soon to become the US
Air Force in its own right) ordered ten pre-production development aircraft, designated YC-97s (Model 367-5-5). The first
example made its maiden flight on 11 March 1947. This aircraft
were virtually identical to the XC-97, but did have revised
engine nacelles for its Wright R-3350-57A piston engines.
Within the batch of ten aircraft there were three distinct build
standards. Six YC-97s were followed by three YC-97As (Model
367-4-6s). The YC-97As had numerous refinements compared
to the XC-97, such as thermal de-icing, hydraulic rudder boost
and nose wheel steering. They also featured the full 75-ST alloy

ABOVE: Identifiable by their side cargo doors, their lack of cabin windows and the
give-away refuelling booms these KC-97Gs are seen still filling the Renton factory
floor as late as 1954 – by which time over 600 C-97s had been built. With Cold War
demand at its peak, finished KC-97Gs were rolling out of the Seattle plant at the
rate of one per day. *Boeing*

ABOVE RIGHT: The C-97 family became the first production-standard USAF
transport aircraft to carry radar as part of their basic equipment. The bulky scope
for the APS-42A radar, as seen on the flight deck of a KC-97G, could be swivelled
between the pilot and co-pilot's seat. Note the relatively clean layout of the main
instrument panel, with white lines grouping related instruments together into easily
identifiable visual clusters. *Boeing*

RIGHT: The navigator had his own dedicated APS-42A radar, as seen here.
APS-42A was first fitted to C-97s in 1950 and was used chiefly as a navigation aid,
through its ground mapping abilities. The radar also had weather functions and
could even detect other airborne targets. This crewman is about to embark on a
pre-delivery test flight and is performing a full pre-flight check on all his mission
equipment. *Boeing*

ABOVE: When refuelling aircraft like this B-50D Superfortress, the KC-97 was well within its performance limits and suffered none of the difficulties of the KB-29s that they replaced. This tanker is one of the three C-97As converted to KC-97A standard, to prove the flying boom refuelling system on the Stratofreighter. These trials were very successful and paved the way for the hundreds of purpose-built KC-97s that followed. *Boeing*

BELOW: The introduction of jet bombers, like this B-47B, brought with it a greater performance differential between the piston-engined tankers and the swept-wing receivers. The KC-97 found itself struggling a little to keep up. This is another early trial involving a KC-97A. Note the nose-up attitude of the B-47 which is pushing the KC-97A along in tail-high position, even though the bomber is throttled back to minimum speed. *Boeing*

structure and extended tail fin that became standard on all subsequent aircraft (and the Stratocruiser). All the YC-97s used Curtiss Electric propellers. The third YC-97A took part in the Berlin Air Lift of 1948 and all three were later modified to C-97A standard for service with the USAF. The last of the YC-97s was the YC-97B, a dedicated VIP conversion. It had no cargo doors and an airline-style cabin capable of seating up to 80 passengers. In 1954 it was redesignated as the C-97D.

The first full production version of the Model 367 was the C-97A (Model 367-4-19), 50 of which were built. These aircraft were fitted with the distinctive chin radome that housed the AN/APS-42 radar, and were fitted with Hamilton Standard props. Three aircraft were modified to serve as KC-97As paving the way for a dedicated air-to-air refuelling version of the Stratofreighter. They were fitted with the flying book refuelling system that Boeing had first developed for the KB-29P. These aircraft were a success in their test and development role, but were later converted back to transports. The C-97A led to the improved C-97C, 14 of which were built by 1951. These aircraft had a strengthened cargo floor and were intended for aeromedical evacuation tasks. 60 KC-97E tanker were built, based on the C-97C airframe.

The main KC-97 versions were the KC-97F and the KC-97G. A total of 159 KC-97Fs were built, followed by a

stonishing 592 KC-97Gs. These aircraft were the backbone of AC's tanker fleet until the arrival of the Boeing KC-135A, in 956. When they were retired from front-line service many KC-97Gs were transferred to Air National Guard units becoming C-97G transports. Some were used by the ANG as tankers and were refitted with J47 jet engines to improve performance. These aircraft were known as KC-97Ls and stayed in service until 1977.

Many C-97s were later converted for other specialist tasks such as electronic systems development (EC-97G), SAR

ABOVE: The dual capability of the KC-97 is well-illustrated by this KC-97G. While retaining its air-to-air refuelling boom the aircraft is still able to carry cargo, in this case a container with a Pratt & Whitney Wasp Major engine inside. The KC-97G freed-up internal volume by relocating some of its fuel to streamlined underwing pods. *Boeing*

(HC-97G), medical evacuation (MC-97C), general test work (JC-97A), engine testbed (YC-97J), VIP transport (VC-97D) and a one-off testbed for a probe-and-drogue refuelling system (KC-97H). Several C-97s were also converted for clandestine Cold War reconnaissance tasks, retaining the outward appearance of regular transports to hide their secret work. These aircraft were particularly active on flights along the Berlin corridors over East Germany.

BELOW: The last serving versions of the C-97 in the United States were the jet-boosted KC-97Ls operated by the US Air Force Air National Guard. The additional J47 jet engines allowed the KC-97s to stay useful well into the jet age, but only just. This Illinois ANG tanker is seen here refuelling an early-production -4C Phantom from Tactical Air Command. *via Walter Klein*

ABOVE: When the 500th C-97 was delivered to the USAF on 5 March 1954 Boeing Model 367 deliveries exceeded Model 377 Stratocruiser production tenfold, and the numbers would keep growing until an astonishing 888 aircraft had been handed over. This particular aircraft was delivered to the 97th Air Refuelling Squadron, at Biggs AFB, El Paso Texas, when that unit began the replacement of its KB-29P tankers. *Boeing*

BELOW: On 18 July 1956 Boeing hosted a ceremony at Renton to mark the roll-out of the last KC-97 and the first KC-135A. Just as the Stratocruiser gave way (largely to the Boeing 707 in airline service, so was the KC-97 replaced by the Stratotanker Both the Model 707 and the C-135 family were based on Boeing's Model 367-80 prototype, which ushered in a whole new era for military and civil aviation. *Boeing*

ABOVE: Out of uniform, several C-97s found their way to the hands of commercial operators who needed the aircraft's heavylift capabilities. Among the best known were the four ex-USAF KC-97Gs acquired in 1969 by the International Red Cross. Converted back to 'C-97G' freighter standard they were used to fly relief supplies to Biafra. *via Carl Ross*

RIGHT: US fire-fighting specialist Hawkins & Powers acquired a number of ex-ANG KC-97Ls for possible conversion to firebombers, but this plan was abandoned *Austin J. Brown/Aviation Picture Library*

BELOW: The last commercial C-97 operators was Agro Air of the Dominican Republic. Agro Air struggled into the early 1990s, and this C-97G is seen landing at Miami in 1988. *Austin J. Brown/Aviation Picture Library*

3 TECHNICAL SPECIFICATION

ENGINES

Pratt & Whitney's R-4360 Wasp Major engine stands as a landmark in the story of piston engine development. Though the first Boeing Model 367 (XC-97) was powered by the Wright R-3350, the R-4360 was specified for the Model 377 Stratocruiser from the outset. It was Juan Trippe, boss of Pan American Airways who saw that his 'ultimate airliner' would only fulfil its true potential when fitted with the 'ultimate' powerplant. The Wasp Major was a radial piston engine that boasted 28-cylinders in a four-row layout. Because of its most distinctive cylinder arrangement, the engine was universal known as the 'corn cob'. Another unusual feature was the engine one-piece crankshaft and split master rods. The engine's norm rating was between 2,650hp (1,977kW) and 2,800hp (2,126kW but for take-off power output could be water-boosted 3,500hp (2,611kW). The Wasp Major was also fitted with turbo superchargers, (see page 46). The R-4360 evolved from th other big piston engines developed by Pratt & Whitney duri World War II. It entered its first phase of tests in June 1942 and b year end was running at an unprecedented 3,000hp (2,238kW).

ABOVE: The Stratocruiser's mighty Pratt & Whitney R-4360 Wasp Major engines provided all the basic power the aircraft needed. However, the real secret of the Stratocruiser's outstanding high-altitude performance was its specially-developed General Electric BH4 turbosuperchargers. The open cowl flaps, required during ground-running, are particularly evident on this BOAC Model 377-10-28.
John Stroud Collection/Aviation Picture Library

RIGHT: 'Sitting Pretty' (according to Boeing), six air hostesses from each of the six Stratocruiser customer airlines 'model' their new aircraft, while still under construction at Seattle. At this time SAS had not yet cancelled its order inherited from SILA. Sitting in the centre-section of the 110ft (33.52m) long fuselage, the ladies lend an excellent degree of scale to the sheer size of the Stratocruiser. The unmistakable 'double bubble' fuselage is also well-illustrated. *Boeing*

PME 15-11267-8

Each of the Stratocruiser's four engines were interchangeable and so could be easily swapped around for maintenance or replacement. This was not a universal feature on aircraft of the Stratocruiser's vintage, and so was a major cause of celebration for the engineers that had to keep the often idiosyncratic engines in service.

When BOAC first took delivery of its aircraft the mean time between overhaul for its Wasp major engines was 600 hours. By the time of the type's retirement in 1958 this had increased to 1,600 hours. Over the same period the propeller overhaul interval had increased from 600 hours to 200 hours.

PROPELLERS

Pan American chose Hamilton Standard fully-feathering and braking propellers, with their distinctive curved section and squared-off tips. These were refitted to the eight AOA aircraft after they were merged into the Pan American fleet in 1950. They replaced the Curtiss Electric electrically-powered

BOVE: The Stratocruiser's flightdeck, or control cabin as it was referred to at the
ne, was a roomy and efficient workplace. The good visibility afforded by
864sq ft (266m²) of window area can be clearly appreciated. The cockpit was
ranged for a crew of five including the pilot, co-pilot, flight engineer, navigator
d radio operator. *Boeing*

BOVE LEFT: Clearly marked as aircraft for Pan American, and Northwest
rlines, this row of Stratocruiser fuselage sections is being joined on the Renton
ctory floor. Forward fuselage sections for subsequent aircraft can be seen in the
ckground. Though the assembly facilities may seem unsophisticated, Boeing
anaged to build all 56 Stratocruisers over a period of just 30 months from July
47 to December 1949. *Boeing*

EFT: Throughout its years of service the Stratocruiser suffered many technical
oblems, some more serious than others. The airlines experienced difficulties with
e Wasp major engines themselves and the new turbosuperchargers, but by far
e most dangerous incidents were caused by the original Hamilton Standard
ops. After a spate of accidents caused by break-away props and damaged
gines, 'Ham Stan' had to redesign the hollow-section steel propeller blades which
d proved so prone to failure. The company drew up four potential new designs
d settled on new hollow dural props. *Aviation Picture Library*

reversible pitch propellers, which had been adopted by most of
the other Stratocruiser customers. All the props were 16ft 8in
(5.12m) in diameter.

The propellers became a source of worry immediately after
the loss of the first passenger-carrying Stratocruiser in April
1952. Propeller failure was suspected as the main cause of the
accident, but not enough parts could be recovered from the
crash area to prove the theory. Other Stratocruisers began to
loose entire props and with them, their engines. On 25 March
1957, following the crash of two Pan American aircraft into the
Pacific (in March 1955 and October 1956) and two further
incidents reported by PAA Alaska Division, the Civil Aviation
Board made some mandatory changes to the oil transfer bearing
design on the Hamilton Standard propellers. The Curtiss
Electric props never suffered any of the same failures and
continued to give trouble-free service.

ABOVE: One intriguing feature of the Stratocruiser was its folding tailfin, a design approach that was also included on the Model 367. The reason for such an innovation was straightfoward — without the folding fin, the Stratocruiser could not be accommodated by the hangars of the day, very few of which had been built for aircraft of this size. This is the Model 377 prototype, seen perhaps on the day of its roll-out, on 2 July 1947. *Boeing*

The problem with the Hamilton Standard propellers lay in their basic construction. The blades were formed from hollow steel forgings filled with sponge rubber, and later, nylon. While there were a very aerodynamic design they were also prone to fatigue cracking. This problem was solved, to a large degree, by replacing the original blades with new sold-core blades.

TURBOSUPERCHARGERS

The Stratocruisers was the first commercial aircraft to be fitted with turbosupercharged engines. Thanks to its General Electric BH4 turbosuperchargers, the Stratocruiser could operate economically at speeds of over 300mph (483km/h) at an altitude of 25,000ft (7,620m). The BH4 worked by augmenting the geared blower of the Pratt & Whitney R-4360 engine — more than doubling its performance at altitude. At 25,000ft the engine would develop 1,300hp (97kW) unaided, but with the turbosupercharger in operation available power was boosted to 2,700hp (2,104kW). Hot exhaust gasses from the engine's 28 cylinders were drawn out by the exhaust system through a nozzlebox into a rotating turbine wheel. This turbine powered an air compressor that drew in outside air through a ram inlet above the engine. This 'turbo-driven' air was compressed, or 'supercharged', then cooled (by an intercooler) and sent directly into the engine's carburettor, where it was mixed with fuel. This fuel-air mixture was next fed into the engine's own gear-

driven internal supercharger where it was further compress and then injected into the intake manifold and back to t cylinders. The amount of supercharged air was varied by simp opening a wastegate bleed valve on the exhaust pipe leading the turbine. The amount of supercharging available was dictat by the power schedule of the engine.

A turbosupercharger (often referred to simply as a turb has several important benefits for the piston engine. By increasi the air pressure in the engine cylinders, a turbo raises the le of available horsepower. Thus an engine can deliver the sar power output at high altitude as it would in the denser air at s level. By raising the cylinder air pressure and using engi exhaust gasses in this cycle, fuel consumption is cut back. T obviously allows the aircraft to fly further on any given fu load. Flying at higher altitudes (thanks to the extra power n available) makes the aircraft faster. For every 1,000ft (305m) higher altitude that the Stratocruiser could reach, its air spe increased by about one percent — thanks to the lower drag the thinner air. There was also a knock-on effect from the ext power provided by the turbo itself.

The BH4 was designed especially for the (mediur altitudes where the Stratocruiser spent most of its time. It w different to military turbosupercharger designs which were usua optimised for higher speeds or higher altitudes. The BH4 w about half the size of a typical military turbosupercharge which were then quite common on piston-engin aircraft. Each unit weighed in at around 220lb (100kg). proved to be a quite demanding design task. The rich hig power fuel mixtures set for commercial cruising operatio resulted in much higher exhaust gas temperatures than we found on military aircraft. Also, commercial aircraft flew long

ₐd more often than military types and so the BH4 had to be a ₑry robust design. Therefore General Electric had to solve a ₐriety of problems to ensure that the Stratocruiser turbosuper-ₕargers would have an acceptable performance and service life.

ᵁEL SYSTEM

ᵀhe Stratocruiser had five groups of seven bladder-type fuels ₑlls — all made from nylon — fitted in its wings. The basic ᵤel capacity was 7,790US gal (6,486Imp gal/29,488 litres). ₑfuelling was conducted through an underwing connection ₙd all the tanks could be filled in about 15 minutes.

ᶜABIN LAYOUT

ᵒeing offering new customers several choices of baseline ₙterior fit for the Stratocruiser. When fitted out in full sleeper ᵒnfiguration on the upper- and lower-decks, The aircraft had ₈ berths, plus another five reclining seats if required. There ᵥere also 14 potential seats available in the downstairs lounge. ₜ the other end of the scale was the high density cabin capable ᶠ seating 100 passengers. In later years some Stratocruisers ᵥere fitted out to carry up to 115 passengers by Transocean. ₗot one of the original five customers opted for anything but ₕe most refined of cabin layouts. The airlines knew that their ₐssengers were all going to be prestige customers and there was ₒ conception that these stately airliners could ever carry some-ₕing as vulgar as 'Tourist Class'! The main cabin was usually

ABOVE: Stratocruiser maintenance was seldom a quick or easy task as the aircraft was fiendishly complicated. In this photograph there are eight men working on just one of the R-4360 engines. However, there was a reason why such seemingly lavish attention was being paid to the BOAC Stratocruiser *Canopus*, pictured here in a Filton hangar during October 1951. The aircraft was being made ready to take the Princess Elizabeth and the Duke of Edinburgh on their royal visit to Canada. *Canopus* enjoyed a particular status as BOAC's VVIP Stratocruiser. *John Stroud Collection/Aviation Picture Library*

fitted with around 65 to 67 seats, plus the additional lounge space (14 seats). The main cabin entrance was located aft, on the port side of the upper cabin. A lower rear cargo door, with a built-in stairs, could also be used to gain access via the internal lounge stairway.

Pan Am had its Stratocruisers configured, initially, for a maximum of 75 passengers, with 53 seats in the main cabin plus two four-seat 'family cabins' amidships. The additional 14 seats were located in the lower deck, but before long, this space was given over to the famed cocktail lounge.

CABIN COMFORT

The Stratocruiser's pressurised cabin was one of its major early selling points. Passenger comfort was also assured by fully-automatic air conditioning and a radiant/convection cabin heating system. When pressurised, the Stratocruiser's main cabin was maintained at a sea-level equivalent altitude, while the aircraft was cruising at heights up to 15,000ft (4,575m). At the aircraft's maximum cruising altitude of 25,000ft the cabin

ABOVE: United boasted about the 'hot food, browned to perfection aloft after its preparation by celebrated Swiss chefs', all part of its Mainliner Stratocruiser luxury service. Meals were served in the spacious main cabin by two stewardesses once they had been 'garnished by the Steward', of course! *United Air Lines via Walter Klein*

interior remained at an equivalent pressure of 5,000ft (1,680m). There were separate cloakroom facilities for both men and women — measuring 238cu ft (6.66m³) and 228cu ft (6.38m³) respectively. By cruising at 25,000ft the Stratocruiser was above most of the worst storm activity found over the Atlantic — which had major implications both for passenger comfort and for overall safety.

PASSENGER ACCOMMODATION

Boeing's Engineering Division made a special effort to develop the seats and sleeping berths for the Stratocruiser passengers. The De Luxe passenger 'day' seats weighed 75lb (34kg) each and had an innovative control panel with a call-bell, reading light switch, an 'occupied' placard, seat number sign, ash tray, and reclining seat controls. Each seat also had a slot into which a dinner tray could be secured. Standard seat pitch was an extremely generous 40in (102cm). The night sleeper seats could be converted into a bed measuring 74in x 42in (1.83m x 1.06m). Furthermore, the private compartments could be fitted with a bathroom, berth and settee. When describing the Stratocruiser's seats, Boeing's press material from the time boasted, 'Whether you are a petite blonde of 100lb or a buxom butter-and-egg man of 300lb you'll be equally comfortable.

The same seat, which supports a 100lb blonde without springing her up into the luggage rack, must be equally pleasing to the 300-pounder without sinking him to the floor.'

CARGO HANDLING

The Stratocruiser had the Model 367 design to thank for its substantial load-carrying ability, but thanks to the fore-sight of Pan American's Juan Trippe the Stratocruiser was one of the first airliners expressly designed to carry cargo as part of its regular passenger-carrying duties. The lower cargo deck had two loading doors, fore and aft of the wing. The forward cargo door measured 4ft 11in (1.5m) across, while the rear door was 4ft 5in (1.34m) wide.

Boeing did once plan to produce an all-cargo version of the Model 377, which it outlined in some of the early press material about the aircraft. This version was intended to have 3,000cu (84.95m³) of usable space and a payload of 35,000lb (15,876kg)

OVE AND BELOW: The most celebrated feature of the Stratocruiser was its lower
ck cocktail lounge, linked to the main cabin by the renowned spiral staircase. It
s features like this that gave the Stratocruiser its 'oceanliner of the skies' appeal.
e mirrored walls, plush upholstery and rather intimate seating had an exciting
nightclubesque feel to it. The lounge area could be outfitted with 14 passenger
seats, and different airlines used the space in different ways. Not all used the lounge
to the most luxurious degree possible, but it still remains perhaps the most fondly
remembered aspect of air travel of all time. *Boeing photos*

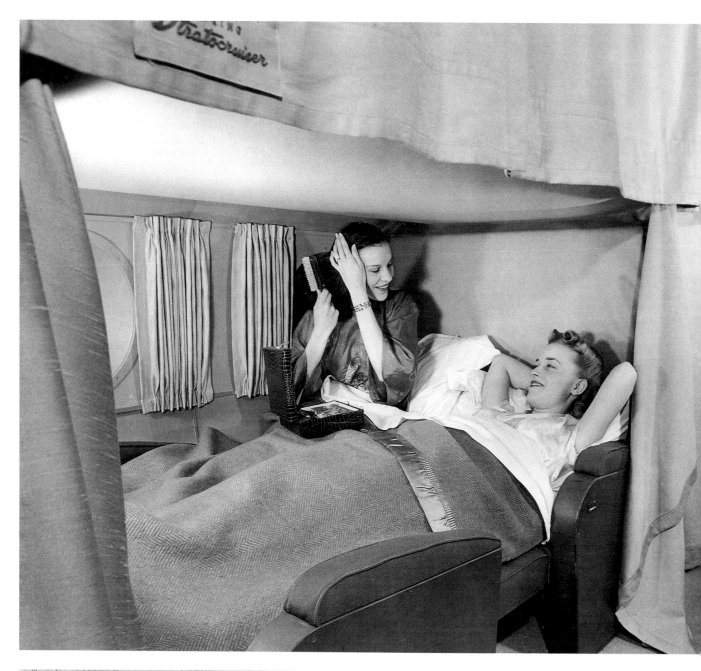

ABOVE: For overnight sleeper services the Stratocruiser's main seats could be folded right down and converted to double beds, if required. Above these lower berths were separate fold-out beds which offered an even greater degree of comfort to the pampered passengers. *Boeing*

LEFT: Boeing was extremely proud of its de luxe cabin seats which it claimed had taken 500,000 man-hours to design and develop, at the cost of many hundreds of thousands of dollars. *Boeing*

FLIGHTDECK LAYOUT

The Stratocruiser was designed to be flown by a crew of fiv with provision for an observer. The pilot and co-pilot sat sid by-side with full dual controls. Their seats were located inboa in the wide noise section. The rest of the 'control cabin', as was referred to at the time, was occupied by a navigato engineer and radio operator. The flight engineer sat directly of the central engine pedestal, where all the engine instrumen were mounted. The navigator and radio operator sat furth back and the cockpit even had its own toilet facilities. The coc pit measured some 680cu ft (19.25m³) with 134sq ft (12.4m²)

ABOVE: The pilot's instrument panel on the Model 377 was simple and uncluttered, with most of the key instruments located on the flight engineer's control panel behind the co-pilot's seat. The Stratocruiser did have a rudimentary autopilot (sophisticated for its time) and the engage/disengage switch for that system can be seen on top of either control wheel. *Boeing*

...vailable floor space. The window glass offered an unprecedented ...ield of view with 2,864sq in (266m²) of glazed area. The forward ...indows were made from electrically-heated Nesa glass, which ...as toughened to resist birdstrikes. The balance of the 19 ...indows were a single plane plastic unit. The navigator had a ...lat-surfaced astral window in the roof, instead of an ...strodome, for which to take sextant readings.

GALLEY

The Stratocruiser's large lower galley was something of a marvel ...or its day. The cabin crew had a fully-equipped flying kitchen ...t their disposal to cater for their passengers. The galley was ...itted with electric oven, refrigerators, more than adequate ...upboard space and vacuum containers for storing hot and cold ...ood and drink. The galley's total area was some 350cu ft (9.8m³).

WEIGHTS AND LOADING

...When the Stratocruiser was certified in September 1948 its all-...p weight had finally reached 142,500lb (64,638kg), allowing an ...crease in the total fuel load from 6,900US gal (5,745Imp gal/

26,119 litres) to 7,615US gal (6,341Imp gal/28,825 litres). With a 10,500lb (4,763kg) payload the aircraft could cover 4,600 miles (7,403km), or 3,000 miles (4,828km) with a payload of 25,000lb (11,340kg).

In June 1950 the US Federal Aviation Administration approved a revised operating manual for the Stratocruiser that permitted an increase in gross weight from 142,500lb (64,638kg) to 145,800lb (66,135kg). This benefited operations from Idlewild, Heathrow and the transit stop at Goose Bay, but not Gander where the runway was too short. Later the weight was increased again to 147,000lb (66,679kg).

FUSELAGE, WINGS AND TAIL

The Stratocruiser used traditional all-metal construction. The 'double-bubble' main fuselage was a semi-monocoque

ABOVE: The level of equipment available in the downstairs galley (another Stratocruiser first) was unprecedented, and allowed the cabin crew to cater for their passengers to a very high degree. Here a BOAC steward is preparing breakfast, in a workspace that would be the envy of any modern airliner. *via William Doyle*

RIGHT: This is actually a KC-97 fuselage section under construction, though from such a view it is virtually impossible to tell whether the aircraft is actually a military Model 367 or a civil Model 377. One clue that it is a military aircraft comes from the lights hung inside the airframe, a sign that the factory was working around the clock on production. Both the 367 and the 377 shared the same fundamental structure, which was buildt to very high standards to ensure the integrity of the pressurised hull. *Boeing*

structure, with an inverted figure-of-eight cross-section specially designed for pressurisation. The aircraft's wing was a cantilever design, set in a low mid-fuselage position. Built around a two spar main section, the wing was covered in an all-metal stressed skin. The skin itself was butted and rivetted into place, with all the rivet joints externally flushed. The wing design used the well-proven Boeing 117 aerofoil section (similar to the B-29) with an aspect ratio of 11.58. Hinges were fitted to the (otherwise) fixed leading-edge sections so that they could be lowered for maintenance access on the ground. The rear flaps were all electrically-operated metal Fowler types and the wing had a built in thermal de-icing system. The Stratocruiser's tail was

RIGHT: In this view of Boeing's Stratocruiser production line the wings, tails and engines have all been put into place and the lead aircraft on the floor are essentially complete. Note the workmen on and around the massive folded fin of the aircraft in the foreground. Note also the very high set of steps needed just to reach the base of the tail section. *Boeing*

BELOW: This series of Boeing design drawings show how the basic Model 367 design, and by extension the Model 377 Stratocruiser, evolved into the jet-powered 'Dash 80' prototype, that in turn gave birth to the Model 707 and the C-135. The full-winged turboprop-powered Model 367-60 proposal, gave way to a swept-wing jet-powered Model 367-64, which incorporated some elements of B-47 design. The sleek lines of the final 'turbojet tanker transport' show just how quickly the snub- nosed Stratocruiser had become obsolete. *Boeing*

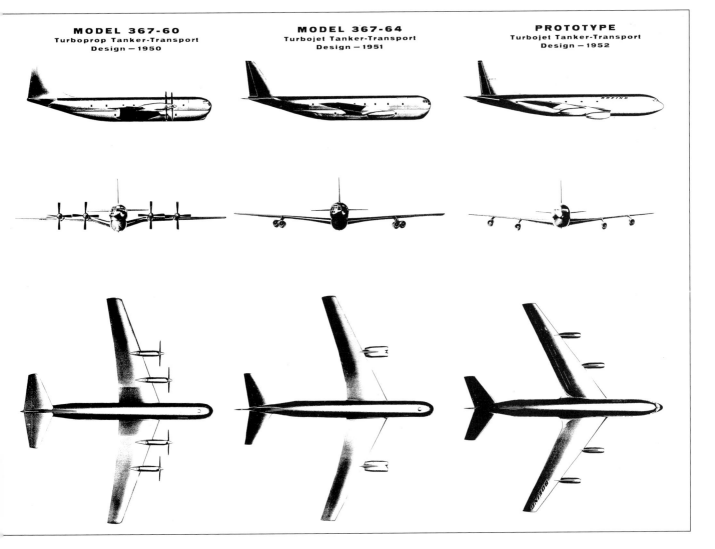

MODEL 367-60	MODEL 367-64	PROTOTYPE
Turboprop Tanker-Transport	Turbojet Tanker-Transport	Turbojet Tanker-Transport
Design — 1950	Design — 1951	Design — 1952

quite a novel feature. It was hinged to fold sideways, allowing the aircraft to be wheeled indoors — as few, if any, of the hangars of the day were big enough to accommodate an entire Stratocruiser otherwise. Once the fin was folded, the Stratocruiser lost some 12ft (3.6m) in overall height. In terms of basic structure, the Model 377's tail was a cantilever monoplane unit with two-spar stressed construction used for all its fixed surfaces. Like the wing it too had a built-in thermal de-icing system. The moving control surfaces all had metal frames, but with a fabric covering (with the appropriate mass-balances and aerodynamic shaping). Trim tabs were fitted to the elevators and rudders. The original fin design was enlarged on the production aircraft to ensure better engine-out handling and to further aid the pilots, the Stratocruiser came with a hydraulically-boosted power rudder.

UNDERCARRIAGE

The Stratocruiser's landing gear was designed to carry heavy military cargo loads and stood as a formidable piece of 1940's engineering. The Stratocruiser used a retractable tricycle layout, with double wheels on all three units. The undercarriage was electrically powered, with a manual handcrank available to the crew in the event of an emergency. The brakes were hydraulically actuated, but they also had a hand-operated emergency back-up in the event of a total loss of hydraulic system pressure. The main (rear) wheels had a diameter of 4ft 8in (1.42m) while the smaller nose wheels measured 3ft (91cm) across. One distinctive feature of the Stratocruiser was its nose-up sit, by about 2°, when on the ground — caused by its elongated nose gear leg. The gear retracted in 11 seconds and extended in three seconds.

SPECIFICATIONS:
Boeing Model 377 Stratocruiser

DIMENSIONS

Wingspan: 141ft 3in (43 m)
Wing, gross area: 1,769sq ft (1,64.2m²)
Tailplane, span: 43ft (13.1m)
Length, overall: 110ft 4in (33.65m)
Height over fin: 38ft 3in (11.66m)
Height, with folded fin: 26ft 7in (8.11m)
Fuselage width: 11ft (3.35m)
Fuselage depth: 15ft 2½in (4.65m)
Ground clearance: 1ft 10½in (0.55m)
Wheel track: 28ft 5.6in (8.62m)
Wheelbase: 36ft 1⅙in (11m)
Minimum turning radius: 29ft (9.85m), approximately

WEIGHTS AND LOADINGS

Empty weight: 78,920lb (35,798kg) to 83,500lb (37,910kg)
Normal take-off weight: 142,500lb (64,638kg), later 145,800lb (66,135kg) then 147,000lb (66,679kg)
Landing weight: 121,700 lb (55,252kg)
Cargo volume: forward hold 520cu ft (14.72m³), aft hold 280cu ft (7.92m³)
Wing loading: 80.5lb/sq. ft (392.8kg/m²)

PERFORMANCE

Maximum speed: 375mph (603km/h), at 25,000ft (7,625m)
Maximum cruising speed: 340mph (544km/h), at 25,000ft (7,625m) at 1,900hp (1,417kW) per engine
Landing speed: 93mph (150km/h)
Rate of climb, at sea-level: 1,100ft/min (335m/min)
Rate of climb, on three engines: 500ft/min (152m/min)
Service ceiling: 32,000ft (9,760m)
Ceiling, on three engines: 21,000ft (8,540m)
Take-off distance, to clear a 50ft/15.25m obstacle: 5,403½ft (1,647m)
Range, with maximum fuel: 4,600 miles (7,360km)

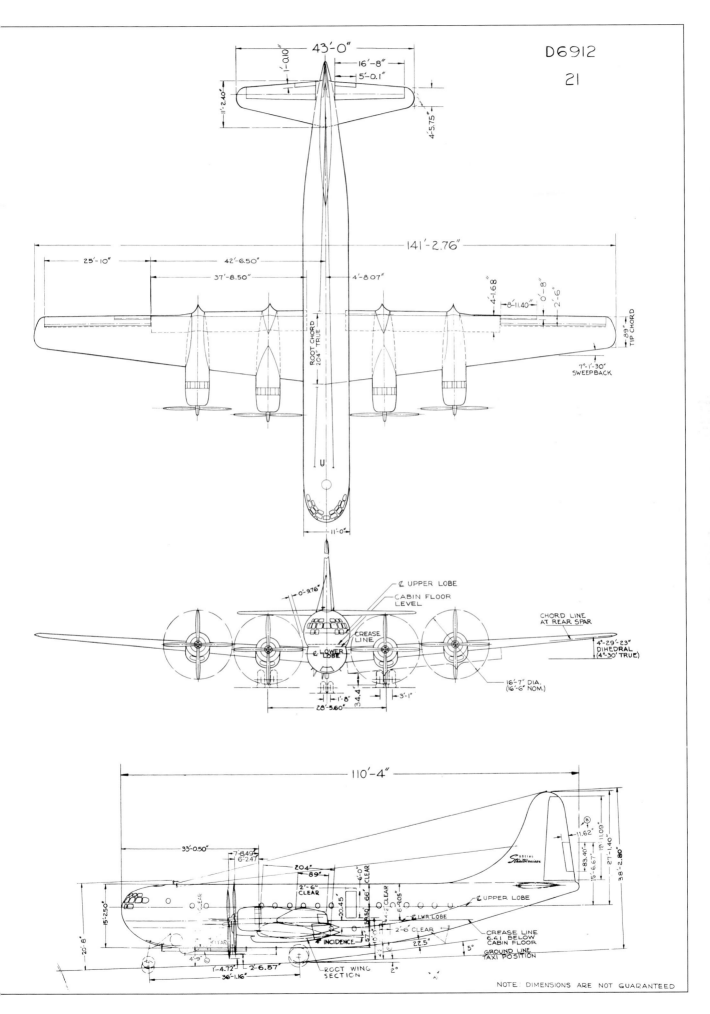

D6912
21

NOTE: DIMENSIONS ARE NOT GUARANTEED

55

4 IN SERVICE

When the first Stratocruiser made its maiden flight on 8 July 1947, Boeing's orderbook stood at 55. Boeing test pilot John B. Fonsaero was at the controls for the first flight and also undertook most of the subsequent flight test programme. There were no obvious problems in the early days of testing, but the Stratocruiser soon proved to be a more complicated beast than anyone had expected. A series of snags and minor problems combined to delay the type certification well beyond its expected date. In fact, it would be almost another two years before the Model 377 was ready for service. This delay was undoubtedly factor in the rapid halt to the flow of orders. The Stratocruiser competitors may not have been as sophisticated or as luxurious but they were available for delivery and airlines began to vot with their feet. For a company used to dealing with far large numbers than 55 this was a worry — but not an overwhelmin one. Boeing was sure that once in service, the Stratocruiser woul begin speak for itself and, to a degree, that is just what happened The Stratocruiser was loved by its crews and passengers and i

BELOW: A private ladies' dressing room was just one of the novel features that arrived with the launch of Stratocruiser services. Boeing described it as a 'glamorously-mirrored powder room in the sky.' Two individual settees were provided, with separate basins and powder dispensers. *Boeing*

RIGHT: With the roar of 14,000 horses behind him, a Pan American line crew chie confers with the flightdeck as he prepares to dispatch the Stratocruiser *Clipper Flying Cloud* (N1028V) for a night-time departure from Idlewild.
John Stroud Collection/Aviation Picture Library

ABOVE: A line up of prospective passengers stand in front of Pan American's *Clipper America*, to illustrate the new airliner's great size and carrying capacity. This photograph was posed before the aircraft was formally handed over — note also the B-29s and B-50s lined up in the background. *via Aviation Picture Library*

RIGHT: *Clipper Flying Eagle* cruises serenely over Tower Bridge, the River Thames and the heart of London on an early visit to the capital. The impact that the Stratocruiser made with the launch of London–New York services — first by Pan American followed closely by AOA — was immense. *PAA via Walter Klein*

fondly remembered by most who flew on it. However, despite all the evidence to the contrary the Stratocruiser eventually gained a reputation for dangerous unreliability. Whatever the facts behind the events, several high-profile crashes began to tarnish the aircraft's reputation and the Stratocruiser would never quite shake the clouds that closed in on it.

With just 56 aircraft ever built it is hard to say that the Stratocruiser was a success, despite all the affection that grew around it. The crashes were one part of the story, but another was the fact that the aircraft did not live up to the bold promises made for it. It was not able to make routine non-stop transatlantic crossings and had to concede to all the same fuel stops that its designers said it would avoid. This was not always the aircraft's fault. Quite often the airports it served simply did not have runways that were long enough to cope with heavy Stratocruisers operating at maximum weight.

Engine reliability was a serious problem — for example, between January 1951 and June 1952 Pan American aircraft alone suffered 60 engine failures, mostly in-flight. These problems were overcome by operating the aircraft at less then optimum cruising speeds and weights. Later technical fixes were implemented that improved the Stratocruiser's reliability considerably, but by then it was too late. With the new jetliners on the horizon any piston-engined airliner's days were numbered. Pan American suffered a particularly bad run of luck and lost three aircraft in three years. A major step forward came when the original Hamilton Standard prop design was changed, and by 1959 Pan

American — the lead Stratocruiser operator — could say that its aircraft were completely safe, reliable and economical. But by then it was too late — the jets were coming.

THE STRATOCRUISER EMERGES

Pan American followed a very deliberate policy of supplementing its existing DC-4 and Constellation orders with 20 Stratocruisers — the aircraft that were earmarked to become the technological superstars of Juan Trippe's post-war fleet. Though the Pan American order was placed in November 1945, the aircraft were not ready to enter service until 1949. On 31 January 1949 and with immense fanfare, Pan American took delivery of its first Stratocruiser (N1025V), which was flown from Boeing Field to Columbia Airport, in Portland, for the all-important hand-over ceremony.

Once again, John Fonsaero was at the controls. Sitting in grand comfort in the aircraft's lower lounge, a senior official from Pan American handed over the airline's final payment for the first Stratocruiser, to Boeing's Vice-President Engineering Mr William A. De Valle. On 5 March 1949, in a ceremony at Washington DC, Pan American's first Stratocruiser was officially christened as *Clipper America*, by Margaret Truman, daughter of President Truman. This aircraft was quickly engaged on a number of route proving trials, to pave the way for the type's full entry to service in the following months.

Pan American flew its first Stratocruiser service on the San Francisco–Honolulu route, on 1 April 1949. On 15 April service

rom New York–Bermuda were inaugurated, and finally full cheduled transatlantic operations to London were launched on ? June 1949 — with aircraft configured for the all-first-class President service. This first flight departed from Idlewild and arried on via Gander to London, launching a three-times a week service by Pan American on the route. Aircraft left the US at 4pm (local) and arrived in London at 10am the following norning. Just eight days after the first scheduled transatlantic ervice PAA launched a once-a-week all-sleeper service. The irline had no hesitation in describing the Stratocruiser as 'the astest, most luxurious airliner ever built.'

One early and unsettling episode for Boeing was the loss of the SILA order. Sweden's SILA had ambitious plans to launch Stratocruiser operations to New York. However, in 1946, SILA joined the group that would establish Scandinavian Airline System (SAS) as the flag carrier for Sweden, Norway and Denmark, and its day-to-day operations were taken over by its rival ABA. ABA had, however, already signed up for DC-6s, but the SILA Stratocruiser order remained on the books and the airline continued to prepare for its introduction into service. In May 1947 plans were announced that Sola airport, in Stavangar, would be the home of the new Stratocruisers. Staff

Above: The Stratocruiser *Clipper Morning Star* (N1042V) was the last of 20 to be delivered to Pan American, in November 1949. Later renamed *Clipper Polynesia*, this aircraft was involved in an incident at San Francisco, on 5 June 1950, where it ground-looped after a gear collapse during landing. *PAA via Walter Klein*

were sent on training courses in the USA and Boeing even dispatched a B-29 to Stockholm's Bromma Airport to ensure that it was capable of handling the mighty Model 377s. The arrival of SAS brought with it new management and new priorities — and the Stratocruiser was not among them. The DC-6 would instead be its long-range airliner of choice. SAS put the Stratocruisers up for disposal and they were acquired by BOAC in April 1949. As a result, Boeing was not left with any unwanted aircraft but it did loose a customer, cutting the Stratocruiser operating base to just five airlines.

THE POST-WAR WORLD

For PAA the post-war years proved to be something of a shock. Pan American had long held a virtual monopoly on long-range routes from the United States, a situation that was almost guaranteed by the strict restrictions placed on its domestic competitors. In the years before 1946, there were virtually no foreign airlines in a position to compete either, and so Pan American became *de facto* America's overseas flag carrier. Things changed sharply after World War II. Suddenly, the US government began to award route licences to the other US airlines which had turned their fleets over to the war effort. In Europe, new national airlines also began to spring up — most of them looking to the transatlantic market with envious eyes. By 1946 Juan Trippe knew that his near-monopoly was under threat, and his greatest rival was clearly Howard Hughes and

TWA. Trippe actually suggested a merger between PAA an TWA in 1947, but he was rebuffed by Hughes. Emboldene by the success of his Constellation fleet, Hughes promised compete with PAA at every turn, and this very public challeng was a major factor behind PAA's acquisition of the Stratocruise in the first place. The situation then worsened, as far as PA was concerned, by the parallel expansion of American Oversea Airlines — the third of the post-war transatlantic US 'majors When AOA became a Stratocruiser customer in 1946, Jua Trippe was faced with the indignity of a rival that was competir with Pan American's 'own' aircraft.

Pan American had ordered its 20 Stratocruisers on 2 November 1945, but a few months later American Oversea Airlines (AOA) weighed in with an order for eight aircraft, o 1 April 1946. AOA thus became the second actual customer fo the Stratocruiser. American Overseas Airlines was born o 10 November 1945 but, as American Export Airlines, it ha been operating war-surplus C-54s on scheduled transatlant routes since late 1945. American Export Airlines pioneered th North Atlantic route and it was an AEA C-54 that made th very first post-war scheduled commercial flight by a landplar — New York–Hurn on 24 October 1945. By September 194

he airline's aircraft had made an impressive total of 15,000 Atlantic crossings.

American Overseas Airlines was a major competitor for Pan American in the early post-war years and clearly intended to challenge PAA's (and TWA's) plans for transatlantic domination. AOA introduced the Lockheed Constellation into service in June 1946 (six months after PAA), and when Pan American's Stratocruisers began to spread their wings into Europe, AOA was not far behind. AOA's first transatlantic proving flight from New York touched down in London on 24 July 1949. On 17 August AOA inaugurated its full scheduled service, with just two aircraft in its fleet. Three flights a week were conducted between New York and London, rising to four by the end of September. In November 1949 the London service was extended to Frankfurt and by 5 January 1950 AOA had all eight of its Stratocruisers in service. AOA had a wider network of routes to European destinations but these remained the preserve of the DC-4 and Constellation.

The Stratocruiser had a worrying effect on AOA's bank balance however and, having made a profit in 1948, the airline plunged into the red in 1949 — the arrival of the Stratocruiser being more than just a co-incidence. Although passengers loved the aircraft, (as reflected in AOA's healthy traffic figures) the operating costs of the Stratocruiser were proving to be too much to bear. AOA was a much smaller company than either of its two US rivals — Pan America and TWA — and it did not have the financial muscle to survive the cut-throat competition. As early as mid-1948 AOA's owners were already in take-over talks with Pan American and in December 1948 the news emerged that PAA was planning a complete buy-out. The competition that had raged between PAA and AOA since 1946 suddenly became hollow. While American Overseas does

ABOVE: RMA *Caledonia* (G-AKGH) was the first Model 37-10-32 Stratocruiser to be delivered to BOAC. It was handed over in November 1949, to become the flagship of the fleet. Shortly afterwards BOAC adopted a new blue and white scheme for its aircraft. *via William Doyle*

deserve credit for being a Stratocruiser pioneer, even before AOA inaugurated its first Stratocruiser services negotiations for a merger, really a take-over, were underway with Pan American.

BRITAIN SIGNS FOR STRATOCRUISERS

Britain's BOAC joined the exclusive Stratocruiser club on 18 October 1946 when it signed for six aircraft to become the core of its new transatlantic fleet. BOAC began services to the USA in September 1946, using L-049 Constellations, but the controversy that surrounded these aircraft was nothing to that which erupted when news of the Stratocruiser acquisition emerged. The Constellations had been seen as stop-gap aircraft which would be replaced by 'proper' British-built airliners as soon as they became available. With its Stratocruiser order BOAC showed that it had absolutely no confidence that such a British aircraft would be available any time soon.

BOAC's Stratocruisers were slated for delivery in 1948 and it is interesting to note that 16 additional complete Wasp Major engines and a further 40 stripped-down engines were ordered with the six aircraft. This purchase represented a considerable investment of scarce US dollars, but BOAC could see that if it did not act, transatlantic air travel would become solely a US preserve. However the delays that slowed down the Stratocruiser's entry into service badly affected BOAC, which had to wait in line behind Pan American and AOA. As traffic grew the airline had no large aircraft capable of taking advantage of this mounting demand — and it soon became clear that six would not be enough.

Some relief came when BOAC negotiated the sale of the four ex-SILA Stratocruisers that were already on the Boeing production line. In April 1949 BOAC managed to buy thes aircraft, using all-important UK currency, and the forme Swedish aircraft became the first to enter British service.

BOAC took delivery of its first Stratocruiser, G-ALSA *Catha* (ex SE-BDP) on 12 October 1949, after its roll-out on 1 Jul *Cathay* flew directly to Heathrow from New York on 1 October. The second BOAC aircraft G-ALSB *Champion* (e OY-DFY) was handed over on 24 October and arrived i London on 28 October. The first of BOAC's 'ow Stratocruisers, G-AKGH *Caledonia*, was delivered on 1 November 1949. The arrival of these three aircraft finall allowed BOAC to begin its Stratocruiser services to the Unite States. The plan was to operate a once-a-week service, vi Prestwick, which would operate alongside the five times week Constellation service.

BOAC knew all about the engine troubles which had badl hampered PAA and AOA's early operations and hoped that i own leisurely introduction into service would help avoid th same experience. The outbound flight from the UK departed o a Tuesday evening at 8pm with a scheduled flight time of 2 hours. The return flight left New York at 11pm EST o Saturday mornings to arrive in London at 07.30am the nex day. The eastbound flight took around 15½ hours — a clea indication of just how much the prevailing headwinds affecte the early transatlantic airliners. On 6 December 1949 G-ALS left London on the inaugural New York flight. By January 195 two flights per week were being undertaken and once eigh aircraft were available a daily service to New York wa launched on 28 February 1950.

On 24 March BOAC took delivery of its tenth Stratocruise G-AKGM *Castor*. Transatlantic services were routing via bot Prestwick and Shannon, though BOAC was keen to promot Prestwick as Britain's own Atlantic gateway. On 23 Apri BOAC launched flights to Montreal, in Canada with a twice eekly sleeper service. By the end of 1950 BOAC had 12 flights week crossing the Atlantic — eight to New York and four to lontreal. In one month alone, September 1950, BOAC's ratocruisers carried 3,678 passengers on the London–New ork route. This was nearly twice the number carried by the rline's Constellations in September 1949.

AN AMERICAN FORGES AHEAD

he news that Pan American was had reached a tentative greement to merge with American Overseas was revealed on 2 December 1948. The announcement shook the whole airline orld — which had already suspected that something was up hen AOA's Chairman, John Slater, resigned a month before-and. The merger process continued to be a difficult one, and nother 17 months of negotiations led only to a rejection of the lan by the United States Civil Aviation Board, in May 1950. hen President Truman himself, not previously noted for any vouritism towards Juan Trippe's airline, stepped in to overrule ne CAB's decision and approve the controversial merger, in eptember 1950. On 25 September 1950 PAA purchased AOA or $17,500,000. The commonality between both airline's tratocruisers made the 'merger' (it was little more than a take-ver) that much more straightforward.

The acquisition of American Overseas Airlines, and its ute structure, gave PAA access to most of the important capital ties of Europe and put it on an even footing with TWA. To egin with, Pan American forged ahead with its Stratocruiser-riven expansion on the New York–London route. It had been oped that the arrival of the Stratocruiser would allow PAA to void the limitations imposed upon its rivals by the early-model L-049 and L-479 Constellations — namely, an enforced

fuel stop at Gander, Newfoundland, before embarking on the transatlantic crossing. In the event, whether the Stratocruiser could attempt a 'non-stop' Atlantic crossing became entirely weather and load dependent. Fuel stops at Gander, and especially Shannon, became a routine part of operations. Pan American discovered that with a load of 35 passengers (or less) the aircraft could fly direct from New York to London. A maximum of 61 passengers could be carried if the aircraft fuel stopped at Gander but only 56 could be brought back. This peculiar equation was due to the prevailing headwinds that affected every west-bound Atlantic crossing, and which forced the Stratocruiser to trade passengers for fuel. The flight time from the US to the UK was about 15½ hours, including a fuel stop at Gander.

On 16 August 1949 — the day before an American Overseas Airlines Stratocruiser arrived in London for the first time — PAA stepped up its own London service to a daily frequency. PAA had launched services to Bermuda on 15 April and, on 1 November, the service was stepped up to one per day. On 5 November 1949 PAA launched its New York–Shannon–Brussels–Frankfurt service — with a total flight time of 17 hours and 20 minutes.

Pan American next turned from the Atlantic to its Pacific routes. The first proving flight from San Francisco to Tokyo was flown, via Honolulu, on 23 September 1949. A full scheduled service on this route was launched on 17 October, with twice-weekly flights. The flying time was approximately 25 hours and

BELOW: As *Clipper Reindeer* and (briefly) *Clipper America* Pan American's N1030V landed at McMurdo Sound in support of the US Navy's regular Operation 'Deep Freeze' deployments to Antarctica. Its first flights to the South Pole came in 1957. *via William Doyle*

RIGHT: United's N31225, *Mainliner Hawaii*, was the first Stratocruiser delivered to the airline and it became one of the six UAL Stratocruisers that were later sold on to BOAC in 1954. Once in British service, the aircraft was renamed RMA *Cleopatra*, and became G-ANTX. United Air Lines had the shortest operational career of any of the major Stratocruiser owners. *Boeing*

50 minutes. Beginning in May 1950, Pan American began to place its Stratocruisers on the San Francisco–Honolulu–Sydney route, which they shared with DC-4s until 7 March 1951. The twice-weekly route to Australia was a marathon journey with aircraft staging via Honolulu, Canton Island and Fiji before arriving in Sydney. San Francisco remained PAA's premier gateway to the Pacific routes, but later services were introduced from Los Angeles, Portland and Seattle.

Pan American returned to its traditional South American 'heartland' with the Stratocruiser in 1950. On the auspicious date of 4 July that year, no less a luminary than Eva Peron christened the Stratocruiser *Clipper Friendship* (N1027V). This launched a through service from New York to Buenos Aires, in Argentina, and Rio de Janeiro, in Brazil. PAA later opened up a route to Montevideo in Uruguay, and in common with its other South American routes the Stratocruisers on this service usually staged through Port-of-Spain, in Trinidad.

BOAC also expanded its services to the Americas when it began a new twice-weekly service from New York to Nassau, in the Bahamas. By January 1951 Stratocruisers were operating three flights each week, and in April BOAC began using BWIA Vickers Vikings to offer a Kingston–Nassau–Montego Bay feeder service to Jamaica. By March 1952 Stratocruisers had replaced Constellations on all BOAC's services to the Caribbean.

By the end of the 1940s Pan American had been joined by three other Stratocruiser operators in the United States, all of which had very different experiences with their aircraft. The first was an all-too-brief Stratocruiser operation by American Overseas Airways. Another relatively brief Stratocruiser user

was United Air Lines, which ordered seven Model 377-10-3[...] on 6 August 1946. UAL was the last American airline to ord[...] the Stratocruiser and from the outset intended to use its aircra[...] exclusively on services from San Francisco to Hawaii. United[...] first Stratocruiser, N31225 *Mainliner Hawaii*, was delivered o[...] 28 September 1949 and by the end of the year five aircraft ha[...] been handed over. The first scheduled service by a Unite[...] Stratocruiser came on 13 January 1950, from San Francisco [...]

onolulu. The flight took an average of 9½ hours, and operated even days a week. UAL operated its Stratocruisers in direct ompetition with Pan American on this route and so rivalry etween the two was fierce. Later that year UAL added a Los ngeles–Honolulu route, one that Pan American did not have.

United had the unhappy distinction of losing the first tratocruiser when N31230 crashed on 12 September 1951. At e time the aircraft was engaged in a training flight and the nly occupants were the three crew, who were all killed. Apart om this sad event, UAL's Stratocruiser operations were without rious incident. Into the 1950s, the aircraft continued to be sed on flights to Hawaii and, in December 1953, services were unched from Los Angeles and San Francisco to Seattle. The tratocruiser never intruded on UAL's wider domestic network, hich was handled by DC-6s and DC-7s, and United obviously und it difficult to make an economical case for the aircraft on nything but long-range high-fare routes. Then in September 954 United decided to withdraw its entire fleet and sell it to OAC. All six surviving Stratocruisers were progressively with-rawn from use and the last UAL service was flown by 31227, from Los Angeles to Newark (pending overhaul for OAC), on 2 January 1955.

The third major US Stratocruiser operator, apart from Pan merican, was Northwest Airlines. Northwest ordered 10 aircraft March 1946 and the company stands out as the only airline use the Stratocruiser over a wide range of domestic routes —

for virtually the whole of the type's service career. United launched the Stratocruiser into service on the Minneapolis–Chicago route on 1 August 1949, with aircraft in a 75-seat configuration. On 1 September the first transcontinental route was opened from Seattle to New York and Northwest soon became renowned for the level of passenger comfort it offered on domestic routes, thanks to its Stratocruisers. On 6 November 1949 services were launched to Honolulu from Seattle, and by 21 December 1949 all ten aircraft were in service.

Northwest operated transcontinental services from Seattle to Washington DC and New York. The Stratocruisers staged through Chicago–Detroit–Milwaukee–Minneapolis–Spokane where they connected with the rest of the airline's route network. On 28 April 1952 Northwest extended its Stratocruiser services to Japan and the Philippines, operating a Seattle–Anchorage–Tokyo–Okinawa–Manila service that had previously been flown by DC-4s. Stratocruisers did not stay on the Far Eastern routes for long, and they were replaced by L-1049G Super Constellations in 1955. The Stratocruisers returned to the US domestic market where they maintained regular services to cities such as Chicago, Detroit, Milwaukee, Minneapolis, New York, Portland, Seattle, Spokane and Washington DC.

To better reflect its widening route network, Pan American renamed itself as Pan American World Airways on 3 January 1950. The name change went almost hand-in-hand with the take-over of AOA, which was sealed on 25 September 1950. Along with its eight Stratocruisers, Pan American took on AOA's network of routes into Europe, which included flights to London, Frankfurt and Amsterdam. Pan American did not re-register AOA's aircraft, though they were soon repainted in the latest version of the Pan American scheme. The arrival of this additional influx of Stratocruisers allowed the airline to open up a number of new routes. The first of these was a New York–Paris service, which was inaugurated on 17 December 1950. Pan American faced stiff competition on this route from TWA and Air France, both of which were operating Constellations. Pan American opted to provide its passengers with the most luxurious service possible and the three-times-a-week Stratocruiser flight became a 'sleeperette' service with just 47 seats. On 2 January 1951 the service was extended to Rome.

LUXURY IN THE AIR

In 1951 BOAC launched its 'Monarch' service between London–New York, which rivalled the levels of comfort to be found anywhere. Passengers could book a sleeper berth and were treated to a seven-course meal *en route* — with champagne and liqueurs served at dinner. The inaugural flight took off on 1 March 1950 and the service soon proved so popular that the three weekly 'Monarch' flights soon became a daily occurrence. In October 1952 the 'Monarch' service was extended to Montreal.

The ultimate Stratocruiser journey was the renowned round-the-word service inaugurated by Pan American in October 1951. PAA had launched the first of these epic airborne odysseys on 17 June 1947, using L-049 Constellations. The round-the-world flights soon became the star item in Pan American's timetable, but the arrival of the Stratocruiser raised them to a whole new level. The 'World Express' became an airline industry superlative and represented the ultimate in chique, luxury and all-round high-living. The Stratocruiser was a more expensive aircraft to operate than any of its rivals, but

the premium that airlines could place on its quality of servi and comfort more than made up the difference. The first-cla (of course) round-the-word service treated passengers to tl finest cuisine from the countries through which they passe Attention was lavished on the travellers by the cabin staff, al the flights also offered a hitherto unavailable way to reach son of the most far flung spots on the globe.

At a time when the world was a far, far bigger place than is today flying around the world in a Pan American Stratocruis had a level of mystique and excitement that is hard to imagir now. Setting out from Burbank Airport, Los Angeles on Friday morning, Pan American flight PA001, better known l its call-sign Clipper One, would spread its wings out over tl Pacific and fly the first nine-hour leg to Honolulu. Stoj followed at Wake Island, Tokyo, Hong Kong, Bangkok, Rangoo Karachi, Beirut and Istanbul before the aircraft reached its fir European waypoint at Frankfurt. The Stratocruiser would the make its way to London before crossing the Atlantic to land New York. Pan American operated these flights in both eas bound and westbound directions.

Pioneered by the Stratocruiser, the round-the-world itinera remained a celebrated part of Pan American's operations rig} into the 747 era. Though it may seem a little churlish, it interesting to note that the round-the-word service did n actually circle the entire globe — flights began and ended c opposite sides of the United States. This was due to a lon standing and out-dated CAB regulation that actually prevente Pan American from carrying fare-paying passengers across tl USA — a regulation that remained in force until the late 1960

BOAC on the other hand earned a prestige reputation fc carrying members of the Royal Family and high-ranking VIP such as the prime minister. Princess Elizabeth flew to Cana for her 1951 royal visit on a BOAC Stratocruiser. In Novemb 1953, this time as HRH Queen Elizabeth II, she flew b Stratocruiser again, to the West Indies as part of her tour of tl Commonwealth. BOAC's G-AKGK *Canopus* was used fc

BELOW: Clearly on a test flight, this United 'Mainliner' Stratocruiser has dropped its undercarriage for the accompanying chase plane. United's Stratoliners enjoyed an excellent safety record, with just one loss — the *Mainliner Oahu* (N31230), which crashed during a training flight at San Francisco in September 1951. *Boeing*

ABOVE: United's Model 377-10-34 aircraft were built with square-shaped main cabin windows, but had rounded windows on their lower decks. Note how the red, white and blue striping across the tail fin is repeated above the Stratocruiser's tailplanes and rudders. *John Stroud Collection/Aviation Picture Library*

oth these flights, fitted out with a revised VVIP interior, and his aircraft was reserved by BOAC for its most important passengers. *Canopus* Prime Minister Sir Winston Churchill and his Foreign Secretary, Anthony Eden, to Bermuda in December 953. *Canopus* next carried Princess Margaret to the Caribbean in 955. Finally, the Duke of Kent travelled on *Canopus* to Accra in 957, becoming the last royal passenger on a BOAC tratocruiser. The prestige that these flights earned for BOAC vas immense and the airline became the sole choice for the wealthest passengers.

A DARK CLOUD DESCENDS

From 1 April 1949 to 28 April 1952 Pan American continued its polished Stratocruiser services without serious mishap. There had been some worrying moments when aircraft had been forced to turn back on several occasions, mostly due to engine problems (*see* Chapter 6), but by-and-large the Stratocruiser vas proving more reliable than its competitors.

The first black day for the Stratocruiser came on 29 April 952, when N1039V *Clipper Good Hope*, travelling from Rio de aneiro to Port-of-Spain fell out of the sky over the Brazilian ain forest and disappeared. After two weeks of intensive searchng the wreckage was found about 400 miles (635km) north-east f the town of Barreiras. The investigators judged that while ruising at approximately 14,500ft (4,420m) the aircraft had uffered an uncontained failure of its number two engine and prop. With the prop and engine vibrating out of control the ort wing failed outboard of the engine nacelle. The tail section, ft of the dorsal fin also broke away — either through collision vith the wing debris or the level of stress on the airframe. The ost engine was never recovered and without it the investigators

could not determine what caused its initial failure. All 41 passengers and nine crew died in the incident.

In 1954 mishaps of a different kind took a hand in BOAC's plans. That year the airline's Comet I fleet was grounded and BOAC was faced with a sizeable capacity shortage. One Stratocruiser was bought from Pan American in August, then another six were taken up from United Air Lines which was retiring the type after only a short service career. The first of these, N31229 (G-ANUB), was handed over on 22 September 1954. Following overhaul and upgrade to BOAC standard in the USA, it was redelivered to London on 9 April 1955. The United Aircraft came with an 81-seat cabin configuration, without any of the dressing rooms or wardrobe facilities of other aircraft, and BOAC retained this to operate 'Coronet' tourist-class services to the USA. The ex-United aircraft were joined by three reconfigured BOAC aircraft — in marked contrast to the 40-seat 'Monarch' class aircraft.

Despite its exemplary record of service and customer care, BOAC suffered the unhappy distinction of loosing the second Stratocruiser to crash on a scheduled flight. This was made all the more poignant by the timing of the disaster, which occurred early on Christmas Day in 1954. The aircraft concerned, G-ALSA *Cathay*, was operating a Heathrow–Prestwick–New York service that had delayed when the original aircraft (G-ALSC) suffered a technical problem on take-off. Passengers were transferred to G-ALSA and they departed from Heathrow at 01.20 on 25 December 1954. The flight was uneventful but

RIGHT: N74601 *Stratocruiser Manila* was the first Model 377-10-30 to be delivered to Northwest Airlines, on 29 July 1949. This aircraft was badly damaged when it over-ran the runway at Chicago-Midway Airport in August 1955. The Stratocruiser suffered a failure in its propeller reversing mechanism and, unable to stop in time, it crashed through the airport's perimeter fence, but no-one on board was injured. *Stratocruiser Manila* went on to have an uneventful service career and like most of the Northwest Stratocruisers it ended its days in the Mojave Desert, in the hands of Aero Spacelines. *Boeing*

bad weather at Prestwick called for a radar-controlled descent to landing. The controller followed normal procedure, talking the aircraft down to an altitude of around 700ft (213m) at which the Stratocruisers crew should have been able to see the ground and the runway ahead. However, the aircraft did not stop its descent and hit the ground about 127ft (38.7m) short of the runway. It ran onto the runway and then bounced back into the air before coming down a second time. The aircraft split in two and caught fire. Only the flightdeck crew (seven) and one passenger managed to escape.

LOSSES MOUNT

It was over the Pacific that Pan American suffered its greatest series of mishaps, loosing three aircraft in three consecutive years between 1955 and 1957. Prior to that one aircraft narrowly escaped disaster when it lost a propeller in flight in December 1953 and made an emergency landing on Johnson Island. On 26 March 1955 Stratocruiser N1032V *Clipper United States* suffered a propeller failure on its number three engine, which then suffered a complete power failure itself. The aircraft was on the first transpacific leg flying Portland–Honolulu, and the engine failure occurred at a point that made it impossible to reach a diversionary airport. The crew decided to turn around and attempt a ditching closer to the US. The aircraft went into the water some 35 miles off the coast of North Bend, Oregon. It was carrying a light load of just 15 passengers and eight crew. However, two crew and two passengers were killed in the ditching.

Another ditching marked the one and only loss of a Northwest Airline's Stratocruiser in 1956. On 2 April 1956 N74608 *Stratocruiser Tokyo* crashed after take-off from Seattle into Puget Sound. Four passengers and one crew member were drowned having evacuated the aircraft safely. Despite having a highly experienced crew on board, the accident investigator found that the flight engineer had left the engine cowl flaps in the open position during take-off, and that none of the other crew members had performed the necessary cross-checks. The captain had attributed the buffeting and loss of control on take-off to a problem with the aircraft's flaps and the real cause of the crash was never spotted.

The second of Pan American's Pacific ditchings, on 16 October 1956, involved former-AOA Stratocruiser N90943 *Clipper Sovereign of the Skies* and became one of the most celebrated feats of airmanship of its day — if not of all time. The Stratocruiser was on a round-the-world trip that had begun in Philadelphia on 13 October. Two days later it arrived in Hawaii and on 16 November it departed on the final leg of its journey. On board were 24 passengers and seven crew. Commanded by Captain Richard N. Ogg, the aircraft took off from Honolulu at 20.26 HST bound for San Francisco. The

estimated flight time was eight hours and 54 minutes. A 01.02hr the crew requested a VFR climb to FL210, which wa approved. Immediately upon reaching this altitude, seve minutes later, the number one engine (port outboard) went in overspeed. Pulling back the throttles had no effect and th propeller could not be feathered, so the engine was stopped b cutting off its fuel supply. The prop continued to windmill an the combination of loss of power and added drag forced th aircraft to loose altitude.

Luckily for the all concerned the US Coast Guard had number of weather ships strung out across the Pacific and th Atlantic Oceans. In the days before satellites they were the onl source of vital weather information — and they also gave crew someone to talk to on the long oceanic crossings. The weathe ships were an essential element of long-range aircraft operation and on this occasion one would save lives. Captain Ogg and h crew contacted the nearby weather station 'November' (th USS *Pontchartrain*), to warn the ship that a ditching was imminen To try and slow the rate of the descent full power was applie

o the Stratocruiser's three remaining Wasp Majors, at which point the number four engine (outboard starboard) began to lose power. The crew managed to maintain altitude at 5,000ft (1,524m) at an airspeed of 135kt (155mph/249km/h). But by then the remaining fuel was insufficient to reach San Francisco or to return to Honolulu. The crew decided to orbit the cutter *November* and wait for daylight to carry out the ditching. At 01.37 the ship began to fire flares so that the Stratocruiser could spot its exact location. At the same time electric water lights were laid down by the Coast Guard crew to mark a track for the aircraft.

At 02.45 the number four engine backfired and failed, but this time the prop was successfully feathered and the aircraft managed to stay airborne on the power of its two remaining engines. For the next three hours the Stratocruiser circled the USS *Pontchartrain* until 05.40 when Captain Ogg contacted the cutter to tell them he was preparing for the ditching and descending to 900ft (274m). The ditching came at 06.15 with full flaps, gear up and at a speed of 90kt (1,03.5mph/166.5km/h). The fuselage broke off aft of the main cabin door and the tail

section fell to the left, trapping a life raft that had been launched from the main cabin door. However the aircraft remained largely afloat and within three minutes all the occupants had been rescued. Captain Ogg's textbook ditching was an unprecedented piece of flying and gained its own form of quiet immortality. By putting his aircraft (safely) into the water he gave birth to a piece of pilot slang that survives to this day — the world 'Oggin' used to describe any large body of water.

This was not to be last misadventure by a Pan American Stratocruiser in the Pacific. On 9 November 1957 N90944 *Clipper Romance of the Skies* disappeared almost without trace while on its way from San Francisco to Honolulu. The aircraft was bound for Tokyo with eight crew and 36 passengers on board. At 01.04GMT, a little more than four hours after its departure, the aircraft made its last routine position report and a search was only launched when the airliner was declared overdue in Hawaii. For five days a large sea and air force combed the approximate area where the Stratocruiser was adjudged to have crashed. The aircraft carrier USS *Philippine Sea* found the

ABOVE: The ever present Washington state landmark of Mt. Ranier, almost a Boeing trademark, dominates this view of Northwest's *Stratocruiser Chicago*. This aircraft was involved in several small incidents, including a fire at Ypsilanti and a collision with buildings while taxying at Cleveland. *Boeing*

LEFT: Northwest's *Stratocruiser New York* waits patiently for another load of passengers. Northwest was unique among the American Stratocruiser operators in using its aircraft across its domestic route network, in addition to prestige international services. *via Walter Klein*

first bodies and pieces of wreckage, some 940 miles (1,512km) east of Honolulu, on 14 November 1957. An actual crash point was estimated for the aircraft, about 105 miles (169km) west of its last reporting position.

This crash was particularly worrying because Pan American had just finished replacing all its original hollow-section Hamilton Standard propellers with new solid props. It was the common consensus that the original prop design was prone to failure. It had been implicated in several of the Stratocruiser crashes, and many more serious incidents. The unexplained disappearance of *Clipper Romance of the Skies* was the ninth Stratocruiser loss, and a particularly bitter blow to Pan American.

Though Pan American suffered several high-profile Stratocruiser losses, these events did not lead to the end of the aircraft's service career. The fact that the crashes were difficult to explain never undermined passenger confidence to the extent that the Stratocruiser became a liability to the airline and its overall service record remained good. In May 1956 (five months before Captain Ogg's Pacific ditching) a Pan American aircraft became the first Stratocruiser to pass the five million-mile mark during a Pacific crossing somewhere between Wake Island and Guam.

The peak of BOAC operations probably came in 1955 whe all the airline's transatlantic services were being flown b Stratocruisers. This included a daily 'Monarch' service to Nev York, and flights to Boston, Montreal and several destination in the Caribbean from London and Manchester (via Prestwick). In July 1951 BOAC introduced its 'Coronet' tourist-class service using 81-seat Stratocruisers, flying to Barbados, Bermuda Boston, Chicago, Gander, Montreal, New York and Trinidad again from London and Manchester, via Prestwick. This was total of 27 flights each week. This does not include th 'Jamaican', 'Bahamian' and 'Bermudian' services that wer flown direct from New York during each week also.

By 1956 BOAC scaled back some of its Caribbean operation handing over the routes to BWIA's new Viscount turboprops Another replacement for the hard working Boeings was comin however, in the shape of the Douglas DC-7C. BOAC began t take delivery of the long range 'Seven Seas' version of the DC- in 1956, to open up new routes to California. By 1957 th Stratocruiser had begun to give way to the DC-7C and BOAC began to redeploy its fleet on services to West Africa. In Apri 1957 a Stratocruiser flew the first London–Rome–Kano–Lagos

ABOVE: The understated markings applied to BOAC's early Stratocruisers nevertheless incorporated the airline's 'speedbird' emblem. *Cathay* would become the only **BOAC** Stratocruiser to be lost. *John Stroud Collection via APL*

Accra. These were in the 40-seat all-first-class configuration, but as more Stratocruisers became available they took over the tourist-class flights also. Two BOAC aircraft (G-AKGI and G-ANUB) were repainted with West African Airways titles over their basic BOAC scheme. They went into service on the Kano–Accra–Lagos route in May 1957, though they were always flown by BOAC crews. BOAC's own Stratocruisers continued to operate their own flights to Ghana and Nigeria, maintaining a daily service via Frankfurt or Rome.

GHANA FOLLOWS NIGERIA

Following Ghana's independence a new national airline was established with BOAC's help. On 4 July 1959 Ghana Airways was founded, with a 40 percent shareholding held by BOAC. A single Stratocruiser, G-ANTZ, was provided to wear Ghana Airways markings and this aircraft launched the airline's new service from Accra to Heathrow on 16 July 1958. In Nigeria, West African Airways was reconstituted as WAAC (Nigeria) Ltd, on 30 September 1958. A number of BOAC Stratocruisers wore its 'flying elephant' logo over the years that followed. The first to enter service was G-ANUC, on 1 October.

Even though BOAC escaped the catalogue of disasters that had plagued Pan American its aircraft did have some lucky escapes and towards the end of their operational careers the aircraft had several brushes with the headlines that, fortunately, did not end in tragedy. On 25 December 1957, a sad anniversary following the crash of G-ALSA three years previously, G-AKGM *Castor* nearly came to grief over the Atlantic. The aircraft was *en route* London–Bermuda, via Gander, when its number four propeller broke way and an engine fire started. After sending out his mayday call, the BOAC pilot Captain Val

Croft was contacted by a Pan American Stratocruiser that was operating on the same frequency. It was being flown by a Captain Gulbransen who had suffered the same problem on a Stratocruiser some years earlier. His advice to Captain Croft undoubtedly contributed to a safe landing in Nova Scotia. On 18 March 1959 Stratocruiser G-ANTY *Coriolanus* suffered exactly the same trouble, also with the number four prop, while flying Accra–London with Captain Croft at the controls again. He made a second safe emergency landing at Accra.

BOAC's Stratocruisers were always immaculately maintained and were renowned as the best looked-after aircraft in service, yet even they were not immune to the Stratocruiser's inherent propensity to cause trouble. The aircraft were now becoming almost a burden to maintain and the cost involved was high. The age of the Stratocruiser was drawing to a close.

The fate of the Stratocruiser was sealed by its high costs and the arrival of new aircraft, ultimately the new jet aircraft. As with BOAC, the long-range Douglas DC-7C began to displace the Stratocruiser on Pan American's signature North Atlantic routes during 1956, and some of the airline's Stratocruiser fleet was reassigned to the Alaska Division. Pan American introduced the Boeing 707 on the New York–Paris service on 26 October 1958. On 19 November the first 707 departed New York bound for London Heathrow (though it had to diverted to Shannon due to fog). The arrival of the 707 was smooth, efficient — and rapid. In the space of a month the Stratocruiser had been effectively replaced in the market that was its *raison d'être*.

ABOVE: Seen here loading freight at London's Heathrow Airport, BOAC's Stratocruiser *Caledonia* served for nine years before being disposed of to Transocean Air Lines in 1958. Like so many other Stratocruisers it ended up with Aero Spacelines, but was written off after a collision on the ground with another Stratocruiser in April 1969. *via William Doyle*

BOAC agreed with Boeing to trade in its remaining fleet of 14 Stratocruisers for 15 new Boeing 707 jetliners. The Babb Company of New York was given exclusive rights to offer these aircraft for onward sale to new owners. The first Stratocruiser to leave the BOAC fleet, G-ANUM, set off for California on 5 July 1958. Its new owners would be Transocean Air Lines and others soon followed. BOAC aircraft remained on the 'Monarch' routes to New York until 13 November 1958, after which they were replaced by the newly-delivered Comet IV. Several aircraft continued service on the African routes, but even they were replaced by Britannias in 1959. On 31 May 1959 BOAC flew its last ever scheduled Stratocruiser service on the Accra–Kano–Barcelona–Heathrow route. G-ANUB and G-ANUC were retained on behalf of Ghana Airways, but the last service for Ghana was flown on 31 August 1959. These two aircraft were not sold on and were scrapped instead, in 1960.

THE STRATOCRUISER'S STAR DESCENDS

It was the DC-7C that began to replace the Stratocruiser in Northwest Airline's service too. The DC-7 had none of the refinements of the Stratocruiser but it was faster and cheaper to operate. By 1959 DC-7s had taken over most of the domestic route network, though Stratocruisers continued to fly Washington–Cleveland–Detroit, Washington–Pittsburgh–Cleveland–Detroit, New York–Minneapolis, New York–Milwaukee and Chicago–Minneapolis services. When Northwest introduced its Lockheed Electra turboprops and then Douglas DC-8 jets, the end was finally in sight for the Stratocruiser. The very last Northwest service was flown from New York to Minneapolis, on 15 September 1960.

The original Stratocruisers did linger for a while in the jet age. Pan American kept its aircraft on the East Coast to Honolulu routes, and the Stratocruisers continued to fly several links in the round-the-world chain — mostly to the airports that couldn't handle the long runways demanded by the new jets. On 17 December 1959 Pan American took the surprising step of re-introducing the aircraft on its services to Auckland, New Zealand. At least four aircraft remained on this route,

flying in from Honolulu via Pago Pago and Fiji. By September 1960 PAA Stratocruisers could be found on this route and just one other — the twice weekly Honolulu–Singapore service.

Alaska was one of the last bastions for PAA Stratocruisers, which were based at Seattle and Fairbanks, but the final scheduled service between the two was flown on 19 June 1960. The very last Pan American Stratocruiser flight was a special charter flown by N90947, from Honolulu to San Francisco. All of Pan American's surviving Stratocruisers were traded in, in exchange for its 707s and most were ferried to Miami, which had long been the airline's technical base for the Stratocruiser. Many were scrapped, but a lucky few were resurrected to begin a whole new life in faraway places.

By the end of 1960 there was a large number of surplus Stratocruisers looking for new owners. However, with a much larger number of more attractive Douglas types also on the market, the Stratocruisers were not an attractive proposition. They were very complicated and expensive to maintain and operate. Their luxurious cachet was of little interest to the type of second- and third-tier airlines that were looking to pick up aircraft on the cheap. Only one company stepped up as a credible operator, the established US supplemental carrier Transocean Air Lines. Other attempts were made to start Stratocruiser services by RANSA, from Venezuela, and LIA, from Ecuador. Of these RANSA was the more successful, but its operations with the Stratocruiser were predictably brief.

The last refuge of the Stratocruiser became Israel, where the Israel Defence Force/Air Force, took up a number of Stratocruisers (and C-97s) that had been specially modified by IAI (Israeli Aircraft Industries). These aircraft fulfilled a number of military special missions roles, and were the last true Stratocruisers to remain operational.

ABOVE AND RIGHT: In the twilight of their careers, BOAC allocated some of its remaining Stratocruisers to help new start-up airlines in West Africa. G-ANUB flew on behalf of Nigerian Airways (West African Airways Corp.) between May 1957 and August 1959. G-ANUC was allocated to Ghana Airways. *via William Doyle*

TRANSOCEAN'S SMALL RENAISSANCE

After the original customers had left the Stratocruiser scene, Transocean Air Lines (TAL) stepped up to replace them. Transocean's roots lay in the pre-war years, but the airline was re-established in a new form in 1946. TAL was a Supplemental Air Carrier, an official US classification given to (smaller) airlines that were allowed to conduct unlimited charter services and a limited number of scheduled services between any two specific points in the US (and later from the US to destinations abroad). The airline earned a rather buccaneering reputation after the war and became involved in a number of operations far removed from the sedate world of the Stratocruiser. Nevertheless when word got out that BOAC was looking to withdraw its fleet of Stratocruisers Transocean found it had an inside track. The company chosen to handle the disposal of the BOAC aircraft, the New York-based Babb Company, was owned by Transocean's parent company the Transocean Corporation. TAL decided to take on the BOAC aircraft and prepared its engineering base at Oakland, in California, for the arrival of the first aircraft.

In July 1958 G-ANUM was ferried from Heathrow to Oakland Airport, to become the first of Transocean's new fleet.

By mid-September Transocean had four aircraft on the US register and was converting them to a new high-density layout. The cabins were refitted with 60 tourist-class seats, 26 standard fully-reclining seats and 12 seats in the lower deck. In a single-class configuration the seating capacity could be boosted to 112.

Transocean's intentions were to launch transcontinental and transpacific services, alongside the airline's three Constellations. The Stratocruisers initially flew a twice-weekly schedule from Oakland and San Francisco to Honolulu, Wake Island, Guam Island and Okinawa, complimenting their already operating inter-island services throughout Micronesia worked by a fleet of four Catalinas (already fed by flights from the US). In January 1959 Transocean expanded its fleet with the addition of two more ex-BOAC aircraft and another four by the end of March. Transocean now had a fleet of 10 Stratocruisers, though only eight were ever placed into service.

TAL operated two weekly flights across the US (in keeping with the restrictions on Supplemental Carriers). From either New York or Hartford, Connecticut, the Stratocruisers flew via Chicago to Burbank, Los Angeles. Services then continued on to either Las Vegas or Oakland. Transocean also offered tourist flights to Honolulu and this became a prime route for the aircraft.

ABOVE: Turboprop-powered Bristol Britannias were among the new airliners tha usurped the Stratocruiser's throne. G-AKGI *Caribou* had the honour of flying BOAC's last Stratocruiser service, via New York, to the Caribbean in December 1958. The following month it was withdrawn from use. *via Aviation Picture Library*

Transocean also attempted to launch transatlantic services, using four 112-seat aircraft on tourist charters to European destinations. During the summer of 1959 Transocean's Stratocruisers appeared all over Europe, arriving in Ireland, the UK, France, Germany and Norway — but these flights were all largely one-offs and the programme was halted in October.

Between April and August 1959, TAL acquired a third batch of four ex-BOAC Stratocruisers — which were all, in turn, former-UAL aircraft. They never entered service, as Transocean was overwhelmed by a series of troubles; the company was facing mounting legal difficulties with its operations in Micronesia which had been ongoing since 1951. Though these flights were being performed under US government contract, the airline was facing increasing legal difficulties because of its Supplemental (*ie* non-scheduled) status. TAL wanted to became the second licensed US transpacific carrier, but these ambitions were continually blocked. The arrival of the Stratocruisers then imposed a major financial strain on the small airline which was not able to expand its business into more profitable areas. Transocean was forced to terminate all operations and declare bankruptcy on 11 July 1960. None of the TAL Stratocruisers ever flew commercially again and its entire fleet of 14 aircraft was sold off for just $105,000.

In South America two small airlines tried to start up Stratocruiser operations. In 1960, Ecuador's Linea Internacional Aerea SA (LIA) acquired one ex-Pan American aircraft with the intention of flying Quito–Miami. The airline failed before the services were launched, and it is unclear if the Stratocruiser ever flew for LIA. Also in 1960, Venezuela's Rutas Aereas Nacionales SA (RANSA) acquired ten aircraft with the intention of converting them to freighters to supplement the airline's existing fleet of C-46s. RANSA's Stratocruisers were fitted with forward cargo doors and the aircraft operated services around the Caribbean and to Miami. Of the ten aircraft that RANSA bought only three ever entered service. The first of these, YV-C-ERH, started flying for the company in October

1961. RANSA's second aircraft, YV-C-ERI, had the honour being the very first Stratocruiser — the prototype NX9070 that had been sold on to Pan American as N1022V in 1950. fourth freighter conversion was underway when the compan filed for bankruptcy on 6 September 1966. RANSA holds th distinction of being the last civil operator of the Stratocruise but that was not quite the end of the story.

THE LAST TRUE 'STRATS'
Looking to augment its limited transport fleet of the earl 1960s, the Israeli Defence Force Air Force (IDF/AF) decide that the Stratocruiser would be a cheap and easily availabl solution. The air force was able to overlook the Stratocruiser high operating costs because the aircraft that it really wanted – the C-130 Hercules — was too expensive to even conside There would also have been inevitable political complication with the acquisition of such a 'tactical' military aircraft fro the US at that time. The sale of five ex-Pan American aircra was brokered by Israeli Aircraft Industries (IAI) and they we ferried from Oakland to Tel Aviv between February and Apr 1962. Little maintenance work was done on the Stratocruiser before their departure and, as a result, they experienced sever very eventful transoceanic delivery flights, and came close t disaster. One Stratocruiser (4X-FOI, the former N90948) h such strong headwinds and ran so low on fuel that a ditching i the Bay of Biscay seemed unavoidable. The aircraft managed t stagger into Bordeaux on two engines with just enough fuel le to taxy off the runway.

IAI undertook a series of freighter conversions on thes aircraft that became the most radical changes ever made to th basic Stratocruiser. The new heavylift aircraft that emerge

ABOVE: A very rare view of three of the 'Anak' freighter conversions operated by the Israel Defence Force/Air Force. Israel took in a total of five Stratocruisers and modified them to act as military freighters. These three aircraft are the ones that did not receive the complex swing-tail modification. *via Lon Nordeen*

ere dubbed 'Anak' (the Hebrew word for 'giant'). Three of the Stratocruisers were modified to *de facto* Stratofreighter standard, with the addition of C-97-style rear clamshell doors, loading amp, internal crane and forward side cargo doors. The other wo aircraft were also fitted with side cargo doors, but they nderwent a more profound transformation. They were each iven a swing-tail, that could be opened out to 92° off the centreline allowing bulky items of freight to be loaded directly into he main cabin.

All of the IDF/AF 'Anak' Stratofreighters could be fitted ith a RATO system and braking parachutes, allowing them to et into and out of the tightest of spots. Though the effort nvolved was considerable, IAI succeeded in militarising the tratocruisers to a high degree and turned them almost into the oor man's Hercules. The basic freighters entered service in 964, while the swing-tails followed in 1965. The aircraft were ccasional visitors to airports around Europe, but were most ften seen in France — Israel's most important military supplier t that time.

It is ironic that having gone to so much trouble to convert ts Stratocruisers into virtual Stratofreighters, Israel then cquired several KC-97s from the USAF in 1967. These aircraft ere converted for a variety of special missions tasks, including lectronic warfare and other shadowy functions. One was shot own by an Egyptian SAM in 1971, but the Stratocruisers ontinued to carry out their important but unsung transport

role. It is ironic too that the aircraft that finally replaced the Stratocruiser in uniform was the same one that had seen it off in the airlines, the Boeing 707. As the IDF/AF began to introduce its (second-hand) 707s in the early 1970s, the Stratocruiser fleet dwindled. IAI did a remarkable engineering job in keeping the aircraft in the air for as long as they did, but by 1975 time was finally being called on the Stratocruiser once and for all. By then, just three aircraft remained in service. The last IDF/AF Stratocruiser — the last active example in the world — was retired in December 1975.

But, amazingly, the story does not end there: the Stratocruiser was reborn at the hands of Aero Spacelines through the remarkable series of Guppy conversions (*see* Chapter 7). Furthermore, one of these ageing giants is still actively earning a living with NASA in the USA. The Model 377 was also outlasted by the military Model 367. The KC-97L remained in USAF Air National Guard service until 1977 and a sizeable number of these aircraft passed into civilian hands. The last examples of former military aircraft remained flying until the early 1990s, used as freighters in Alaska and around Central America and the Caribbean — but they are all gone now, and the sound of their mighty R-4360s is no more.

5 OPERATORS

PAN AMERICAN WORLD AIRWAYS (PAA)

PAA was the launch customer for the Stratocruiser and was the first airline to put the new Boeing into service (closely followed by its first Lockheed 049 Constellations). On 28 November 1945 Pan American signed a deal for 20 Stratocruisers, valued at $25 million. At the time this was cited as the largest ever placed order for commercial aircraft. With all the work that had been completed on the military Model 367 Pan Am and Boeing hoped that the airline would be able to place its Model 377s into commercial service by the end of 1946. However, the Model 377 certification process became far more drawn out than either party expected and so the first PAA Stratocruisers did not enter service until 1949.

Pan American took delivery of its first aircraft, N1025V which became *Clipper America*, on 31 January 1949. This aircraft was immediately set to work on several route-proving trials, mainly on the San Francisco–Honolulu run. The second PAA Stratocruiser to be delivered was N1026V, which arrived on 17 February 1949. It was followed by the third example, N1027V, on 2 March 1949. Pan American's fourth aircraft was N1028V, on 14 March 1949, with the fifth aircraft, N1023V, handed over on 19 March 1949. Pan American's sixth Stratocruiser was

ABOVE: Pan American's first Stratocruisers were delivered in an overall natural metal finish, with cheat-lines and other markings. This particular aircraft later we on to serve as the baseline airframe for the Aero Spacelines Pregnant Guppy conversion, in 1962. *via Aviation Picture Library*

N1030V (delivered 30 March 1949) and its seventh wa N1029V (delivered 22 April 1949). The first productio Stratocruiser, N1024V, was retained by Boeing for it own in house trials and was not handed over to Pan American until 1 June 1949, becoming the airline's tenth example. By the end o their operational careers Pan American had configured it Stratocruisers in an 86-seat layout, while the former AOA aircraft were in a similar 81-seat all-tourist configuration.

ABOVE RIGHT: The last colour scheme worn by Pan American's Stratocruisers wa the jet-era livery introduced on the first Boeing 707s. It looked very out of place on the elderly propliners. *Stephen Piercey/Aviation Picture Library*

BELOW: *Clipper Washington* shows off the revised scheme applied to PAA Stratocruisers, which began to appear after the airline changed its name to Pan American World Airways. This new livery incorporated a white fuselage top with large blue titles on the fin. As with most Pan American colour schemes, many aircraft displayed slight differences to this basic design. *via Walter Klein*

PAN AMERICAN WORLD AIRWAYS (PAA) FLEET

Con. No.	Model	Reg.	Name	Notes
15923	377-10-26	N1023V	Clipper Golden Gate	crashed 2 June 1958
15924	377-10-26	N1024V	Clipper Bald Eagle	later Clipper Cathay. to Aero Spacelines, N126AJ
15925	377-10-26	N1025V	Clipper America	later Clipper Rainbow, Clipper Celestial. to IAI, IDF/AF
15926	377-10-26	N1026V	Clipper Tradewind	later Clipper Malay. to RANSA
15927	377-10-26	N1027V	Clipper Friendship	to BOAC (G-ANUM)
15928	377-10-26	N1028V	Clipper Flying Cloud	to RANSA (YV-C-ERJ)
15929	377-10-26	N1029V	Clipper Golden Eagle	to RANSA
15930	377-10-26	N1030V	Clipper Southern Cross	later Clipper Reindeer, Clipper America. to IAI, IDF/AF
15931	377-10-26	N1031V	Clipper Mayflower	later Clipper Donald McKay. to RANSA (YV-C-ERH)
15932	377-10-26	N1032V	Clipper United States	crashed 26 March 1955
15933	377-10-26	N1033V	Clipper Seven Seas	later Clipper Midnight Sun. crashed 10 April 1959
15934	377-10-26	N1034V	Clipper Westward Ho	to RANSA (YV-C-ERK)
15935	377-10-26	N1035V	Clipper Flying Eagle	to RANSA
15936	377-10-26	N1036V	Clipper Washington	to RANSA
15937	377-10-26	N1037V	Clipper Fleetwing	to Aero Spacelines, Super Guppy
15938	377-10-26	N1038V	Clipper Constitution	later Clipper Hotspur. to Aero Spacelines, Super Guppy
15939	377-10-26	N1039V	Clipper Good Hope	crashed 29 April 1952
15940	377-10-26	N1040V	Clipper Invincible	to LIA (HC-AFS)
15941	377-10-26	N1041V	Clipper Yankee	later Clipper Northern Light. broken up
15942	377-10-26	N1042V	Clipper Morning Star	later Clipper Polynesia. to Aero Spacelines, broken up
15922	377-10-26	N1043V	Clipper Nightingale	delivered October 1950, previously 377-10-19 prototype (NX90700) to RANSA (YV-C-ERI)
15957	377-10-29	N90941	Clipper America	later Clipper Australia. formerly AOA dbr in landing accident 9 July '59
15958	377-10-29	N90942	Clipper Glory of the Skies	formerly AOA, to Aero Spacelines
15959	377-10-29	N90943	Clipper Sovereign of the Skies	formerly AOA, to RANSA
15960	377-10-29	N90944	Clipper Romance of the Skies	formerly AOA, crashed 9 November 1957
15961	377-10-29	N90945	Clipper Monarch of the Skies	formerly AOA, to RANSA
15962	377-10-29	N90946	Clipper Queen of the Skies	formerly AOA, to IAI, IDF/AF
15963	377-10-29	N90947	Clipper Good Hope	later Clipper Queen of the Pacific. formerly AOA to IAI, IDF/AF
15964	377-10-29	N90948	Clipper Eclipse	later Clipper Mandarin. formerly AOA, to IAI, IDF/AF

SILA
(SVENSK INTERCONTINENTAL LUFTTRAFIK AB)

The Scandinavian Airline SILA was one of the forerunners of today's SAS and it followed PAA's lead to become the second customer for the Stratocruiser. In February 1946 SILA signed an agreement to purchase four aircraft, valued at $6 million. SILA hoped to use these aircraft to open up direct services between Stockholm and New York, beginning in 1947. However, the lengthy delays in the Stratocruiser certification programme led to a major change of plan. The SILA aircraft entered production and were to be outfitted with a sumptuous interior using all-Swedish fabric and materials. But as the aircraft moved along the Renton line SILA underwent a change of ownership. In July 1946 the airline became one of the founders of the Scandinavian Airline System, but its operations were taken over by Sweden's AB Aerotransport.

ABA was already committed to the Douglas DC-6, though SAS never cancelled its Stratocruiser order. SAS finally decided to dispose of the four SILA aircraft and, in April 1949, it sold them to BOAC. For BOAC this was a much-welcomed boost in capacity and allowed the British airline to start up its Stratocruiser services much earlier than would otherwise have been the case.

SILA Fleet

Con. no.	Model	Reg.	Notes
15943	377-10-28	SE-BDP	later G-ALSA, BOAC
15944	377-10-28	OY-DF	later G-ALSB, BOAC
15945	377-10-28	LN-LAF	later G-ALSC, BOAC
15946	377-10-28	SE-BDR	later G-ALSD, BOAC

AMERICAN OVERSEAS AIRLINES (AOA)

AOA became the third Stratocruiser customer when it placed an order for ten aircraft on 1 April 1946. AOA was actually founded as American Export Airlines by a shipping company, American Export Lines, in 1942. The airline (AEA) had begun transatlantic services with Vought-Sikorsky VS-44 flying boats, but under contract to the US Navy's Air Transport Services.

Immediately after the war AEA merged with American Airlines Inc. (Overseas Division) to became American Overseas Airlines. In fact, it was AOA that made the first commercial flight from the US to Britain after World War II, arriving in Bournemouth's Hurn Airport on 24 October 1945. AOA was a well-established challenger to Pan American and Transcontinental & Western Airlines (TWA) on the transatlantic routes. This was underlined by its Stratocruisers which were intended to take on Pan American head-to-head.

ABOVE: American Overseas' Stratocruisers had a short but eventful career before the airline and its aircraft were consumed by Pan American, in 1950. *Boeing*

The AOA Model 377-10-29 Stratocruisers were notable for their circular upper deck windows, rectangular lower deck windows and their Curtiss Electric propellers. The first aircraft, N90941, was rolled out on 23 February 1949, made its first flight on 15 March and was delivered to the airline on 13 June. American Overseas carried out its plans for a network of Stratocruiser services from the US to Europe and followed Pan American onto the New York to London route in just six weeks. By 1948 AOA's owners were in heavy discussion with Juan Trippe and protracted negotiations eventually did lead to Pan American take-over of AOA on 25 September 1950. AOA Stratocruisers were soon absorbed into the Pan American fleet taking it up to a total of 29.

AMERICAN OVERSEAS AIRWAYS FLEET

CON. NO.	MODEL	REG.	NAME	NOTES
15957	377-10-29	NC90941, N90941	*Flagship Great Britain*	later *Flagship Europe, Flagship Scandinavia* to PAA
15958	377-10-29	NC90942, N90942	*Flagship Europe*	later *Flagship Great Britain* to PAA
15959	377-10-29	NC90943, N90943	*Flagship Holland*	later *Flagship Europe* to PAA
15960	377-10-29	NC90944, N90944	*Flagship Ireland*	to PAA
15961	377-10-29	NC90945, N90945	*Flagship Norway*	to PAA
15962	377-10-29	NC90946, N90946	*Flagship Sweden*	to PAA
15963	377-10-29	NC90947, N90947	*Flagship Denmark*	to PAA
15964	377-10-29	NC90948, N90948	*Flagship Scotland*	to PAA

NORTHWEST AIRLINES

Northwest was the fourth Stratocruiser customer, placing an order for ten Model 377-10-30 aircraft in March 1946. Northwest's aircraft were fitted with Hamilton Standard propellers and had rectangular cabin windows. The first aircraft, N74601, was rolled out on 18 February 1949, but the first to be delivered to the airline was N74602, on 22 June 1949. This aircraft was named *Stratocruiser Minneapolis St Paul* — in honour of Northwest's main hub of operations, which remains so to this day. The first commercial service was flown from Minneapolis to Chicago on 1 August 1949. Northwest was alone among the original Stratocruiser operators in configuring its aircraft in a 'higher-density' 75-seat layout. Despite this, Northwest's Stratocruisers became renowned for their level of passenger service and it was the only airline able to offer

ABOVE: Apart from the addition of small 'Orient' titles to the main legend, Northwest Airlines' Stratocruisers changed very little in appearance over the years. The red wing tips, and large titles over the wings, left little doubt as to the aircraft's ownership, when seen from any angle. *Boeing*

Stratocruiser-class comfort on US trunk routes. Northwest's tenth and final Stratocruiser was delivered on 21 December 1949. This aircraft was named *Stratocruiser The Orient Express* by the actress Loretta Young, as part of the promotional effort surrounding her new film *Keys to the City*.

Northwest suffered just one loss of an aircraft during its Stratocruiser years, when N74608 crashed in Puget Sound in 1956. The withdrawal of the Stratocruiser fleet began in 1959 when Northwest began to transition first to Douglas DC-7s and then to Lockheed Electras and Douglas DC-8s. The eight surviving Stratocruisers were traded in to Lockheed in exchange for a new fleet of L-188 Electras. One of these Stratocruisers (N74607) had been badly damaged by an internal fire caused by an exploding oxygen bottle on 14 July 1959. This aircraft was later sold on to RANSA for spares. The last Northwest

Airlines Stratocruiser service was operated on 15 Septemb 1960. The aircraft were eventually sold to Lee Mansdorf ar several were used by Aero Spacelines for the Guppy conversion

NORTHWEST AIRLINES FLEET

CON. NO.	MODEL	REG.	NAME	NOTES
15947	377-10-30	NC74601, N74601	Stratocruiser Manila	to Aero Spacelines
15948	377-10-30	NC74602, N74602	Stratocruiser Minneapolis-St Paul	to Aero Spacelines
15949	377-10-30	NC74603, N74603	Stratocruiser New York	to Aero Spacelines
15950	377-10-30	NC74604, N74604	Stratocruiser New York	later Detroit, to Aero Spacelines
15951	377-10-30	NC74605, N74605	Stratocruiser Chicago	later Newark, to Aero Spacelines
15952	377-10-30	NC74606, N74606	Stratocruiser Washington	to Aero Spacelines
15953	377-10-30	NC74607, N74607	Stratocruiser Honolulu	later Rudolph dbr 14/8/59, broken up for spares
15954	377-10-30	NC74608, N74608	Stratocruiser Tokyo	later Newark, crashed 2/4/56
15955	377-10-30	NC74609, N74609	Stratocruiser Alaska	later Portland, to Aero Spacelines
15956	377-10-30	NC74610, N7461	Stratocruiser The Orient Express	later Shanghai, Formosa to Aero Spacelines

BRITISH OVERSEAS AIRWAYS CORPORATION

In September 1946 BOAC announced its intention to acquire the Stratocruiser, becoming the sixth and last of the original Model 377 customers. This purchase became highly controversial in cash-strapped post-war Britain, with many questioning why the national carrier was choosing to spend so much scarce foreign currency on American aircraft and not instead supporting domestic industry. The truth of the matter was that there was no home-grown option for BOAC and none would be available until the advent of the Bristol Britannia, many years later. BOAC knew that it could not leave the new transatlantic market as the sole preserve of the United States and so it had no choice but to order the Stratoliner .

The formal order for six Model 377-10-32 aircraft was agreed on 18 October 1946. BOAC then did a deal with SAS which still held rights to the four Model 377-10-28 Stratocruisers that had been ordered by SILA. These aircraft were now unwanted, but were already being built and would be available sooner than any of BOAC's own Stratoliners. The four

ABOVE: The first four Stratocruisers delivered to BOAC were the one-time SILA aircraft and they provided a much-welcomed boost for BOAC in the race to establish transatlantic services. G-ALSA entered revenue service on the London–Prestwick–New York service on 6 December 1949. In 1954 the aircraft wa damaged in a heavy landing at Keflavik, then later crashed at Prestwick. via APL

aircraft were bought in April 1949 and the first was rolled ou at Renton on 1 July 1949. This was G-ALSA (the one-tim SE-BDP) which was named Cathay. She was handed over in ceremony at Seattle on 12 October and arrived in London on 1 October. The SILA -28 aircraft had some differences t BOAC's -32s. The galley was positioned amidships in the -28 while the -32s had an aft galley. The -28s had circular window on the upper and lower decks, while the BOAC -32s had squar windows on the lower deck.

BOAC's Stratocruisers were given names that had once bee carried by the great Short 'C' Class flying boats of Imperi Airways. This was prefixed by 'RMA' — Royal Mail Aircraft.

By 24 March 1950 all ten of BOAC's initial batch o Stratocruisers had been delivered — the last to arrive wa

ABOVE: seen here at BOAC's base of operations at Heathrow, G-ANUC *Clio* was one of the Model 377-10-34 aircraft obtained from United Airlines. *Clio* is painted in the white-topped scheme adopted by BOAC to favour the all-metal finish.

RIGHT: The final scheme worn by BOAC's Stratocruisers featured a dark blue tail with a white speedbird — a negative image of the previous blue-on-white finish. This aircraft, G-ALSD *Cassiopeia*, was the last of our -28 Stratocruisers acquired by BOAC in late 1949.

G-AKGM *Castor*. These aircraft were fitted out with 60 first-class seats, arranged in three defined cabins that were separated by the galley amidships. The cabins were laid out for eight, 24 and 28 passengers from fore to aft. A dumb-waiter ran from the galley to the downstairs lounge. In all-sleeper configuration the aircraft were usually fitted with 24 berths and 28 reclining sleeper seats. For the 'Monarch' services, introduced in early 1950, seven aircraft (G-AKGH, G-AKGI, G-AKGJ, G-ALSA, G-ALSB, G-ALSC and G-ALSD) were reconfigured with 40 seats.

In 1954 BOAC's de Havilland Comet I jet fleet was grounded and the airline was faced with a large and very unexpected capacity shortage. BOAC decided to add to its Stratocruiser fleet and acquired a single Model 377-10-26 aircraft (N1027V) from Pan American on 26 August 1954. This aircraft was fitted out in the 40-seat 'Monarch' layout. Another six aircraft were soon acquired from United Air Lines which had begun to dispose of its Stratocruiser fleet. The first of these, N31229 (G-ANUB), was handed over on 22 September 1954. Following overhaul and upgrade to BOAC standard in the USA, it was redelivered to London on 9 April 1955. The sixth and final ex-UAL Model 377-10-34 was delivered to Heathrow on 15 June

1955. The United aircraft could be easily recognised by their square upper deck windows and the circular windows on the lower deck. Unlike the other BOAC Stratoliners, the ex-United aircraft were in an 81-seat all-tourist layout and they were soon joined by three of BOAC's own aircraft (G-AKGK, G-AKGL and G-AKGM) in the same configuration. These aircraft were used on the transatlantic 'Coronet' tourist services. On some services to the Caribbean, BOAC operated a 'mixed' configuration of 50 tourist seats in the forward cabin, along with ten sleeper seats and 13 sleeping berths aft.

Beginning in July 1958 BOAC began to dispose of its Stratocruisers, via the Babb Company of New York which had been chosen by Boeing to act as brokers for the second-hand Stratocruiser fleet. The first aircraft to be retired was G-ANUM, which left the fleet on 5 August 1958. This aircraft was subsequently redelivered to Transocean Air Lines, along with five other ex-BOAC Stratocruisers. During ten years of operations BOAC's aircraft had carried 680,000 passengers over 12,804 Atlantic crossings and 247,500 flying hours. All but one had undertaken 1,000 Atlantic crossings and G-AKGL led the fleet with 1,161 to its credit.

BRITISH OVERSEAS AIRWAYS CORPORATION FLEET

CON. NO.	MODEL	REG.	NAME	NOTES
15974	377-10-32	G-AKGH	Caledonia	became N137A, Transocean
15975	377-10-32	G-AKGI	Caribou	became N100Q, Transocean
15976	377-10-32	G-AKGJ	Cambria	became N102Q, Transocean
15977	377-10-32	G-AKGK	Canopus	became N105Q, Transocean
15978	377-10-32	G-AKGL	Cabot	became N85Q, Transocean
15979	377-10-32	G-AKGM	Castor	became N104Q, Transocean
15943	377-10-28	G-ALSA	Cathay	formerly SE-BDP (SILA), crashed 25 December 1954
15944	377-10-28	G-ALSB	Champion	formerly OY-DFY (SILA), later N103Q, Transocean
15945	377-10-28	G-ALSC	Centaurus	formerly LN-LAF (SILA), later N101Q, Transocean
15946	377-10-28	G-ALSD	Cassiopeia	formerly SE-BDR (SILA), later N86Q, Transocean
15965	377-10-34	G-ANTX	Cleopatra	formerly N31225 (UAL), later N107Q, Transocean
15966	377-10-34	G-ANTY	Coriolanus	formerly N31226 (UAL), later N108Q, Transocean
15967	377-10-34	G-ANTZ	Cordellia	formerly N31227 (UAL), later N106Q, Transocean
15968	377-10-34	G-ANUA	Cameronian	formerly, N31228 (UAL), later N109Q, Transocean
15969	377-10-34	G-ANUB	Calypso	formerly N31229 (UAL)
15971	377-10-34	G-ANUC	Clio	formerly N31231 (UAL)
15927	377-10-26	G-ANUM	Clyde	formerly N1027V (PAA)

UNITED AIR LINES

United joined PAA, AOA and Northwest to become the fifth Stratocruiser customer. United ordered seven Model 377-10-34 Stratocruisers on 6 August 1946 and these aircraft were earmarked to serve on the first-class routes from California to Hawaii. The first UAL Stratocruiser, N31225, was delivered on 28 September 1949.

This aircraft began a series of crew training and route proving flights. By the end of 1949 United had five aircraft in its fleet and was preparing to place the type into service. Services to Honolulu from San Francisco were launched on 13 January 1950 and the Stratocruisers replaced DC-6s on the route. UAL's aircraft were configured in a 55-seat sleeper layout and had all the creature comforts that Stratocruiser passengers had come to expect, including the ubiquitous cocktail lounge. United was the shortest lived of all the major Stratocruiser operators. UAL's six remaining Stratocruisers were sold to BOAC in 1954.

ABOVE AND RIGHT: United's *Mainliner Hawaii* served for just over five years before it became BOAC's RMA *Cleopatra*. The aircraft is seen here on a pre-delivery test flight, wearing United's distinguished livery. In common with the aircraft of many other airlines of the time, United's Stratocruisers adopted large company titles on the wing, alongside over-sized registrations that allowed the aircraft to be easily identified. *John Stroud Collection/ Aviation Picture Library and Boeing*

LEFT: **G-AKGK** *Canopus* served with BOAC from February 1950 until March 1959. Like many BOAC Stratocruisers *Canopus* was acquired by Transocean Air Lines, via the Babb Company, when BOAC began to dispose of its Stratocruiser fleet. It was later bought by Aero Spacelines, and was finally scrapped in 1969. *via Aviation Picture Library*

UNITED AIR LINES FLEET

CON. NO.	MODEL	REG.	NAME	NOTES
15965	377-10-34	NC31225, N31225	*Mainliner Hawaii*	to BOAC (G-ANTX)
15966	377-10-34	NC31226, N31226	*Mainliner Kauai*	to BOAC (G-ANTY)
15967	377-10-34	NC31227, N31227	*Mainliner Hana Maui*	to BOAC (G-ANTZ)
15968	377-10-34	NC31228, N31228	*Mainliner Waipahu*	later to BOAC (G-ANUA)
15969	377-10-34	NC31229, N31229	*Mainliner Hilo*	to BOAC (G-ANUB)
15970	377-10-34	NC31230, N31230	*Mainliner Oahu*	crashed 12/9/51
15971	377-10-34	NC31231, N31231	*Mainliner Kano*	to BOAC (G-ANUC)

TRANSOCEAN AIR LINES

Transocean started life as a non-scheduled and contract carrier. The company was founded by Orvis M. Nelson, a former senior United Air Lines pilot. Transocean made a sizeable mark when it handled the transfer of over 150 war surplus Curtiss C-46s from the US to China, in 1946. Despite expectations to the contrary, Transocean did not loose a single aircraft during this operation. The airline then became involved in operations around the world, flying immigrants from the UK to Canada in 1947 and conducting transport operations during the Korean War.

Transocean began to take delivery of ex-BOAC Stratocruisers in 1958 and the first four aircraft were ferried to the company base at Oakland Airport, California. On 5 July,

BOAC's former flagship, G-AKGH was transferred to TAL. It was followed, in August, by G-AKGH. G-ALSD and G-AKGL were delivered on 7 and 13 September, respectively. A new technical centre was established at Bradley Field, Connecticut, where Transocean intended to base its new Atlantic Coast engineering division. All of the aircraft were refitted with a revised seating layout that could accommodate between 98 (two-class) and 112 (single-class) passengers. These aircraft used a range of US registrations for their ferry flights and initial operations, they were later re-registered in the N4**Q series, starting at N401Q.

A second batch of six aircraft was acquired in 1959, with G-ALSC delivered on 5 January and G-AKGI delivered on

6 January. By the end of March another four had been handed over (G-AKGJ, G-ALSB, G-AKGK, G-AKGM). Only four of these aircraft would ever enter service — as N405Q, N406Q, N409Q and N410Q. TAL's final batch of four ex-BOAC aircraft was delivered between April and August 1959. These were all, in turn, former United Airlines aircraft. Although all were registered, none ever entered service with Transocean.

On 1 July 1951 the company was awarded a contract by the US Department of the Interior to undertake contracted air services across Micronesia (the Marshall, Caroline and Marian Islands) for which Transocean acquired a fleet of four PBY-5 Catalinas. The legal difficulties that surrounded a non-scheduled airline conducting a scheduled network of services eventually overwhelmed Transocean and the company was forced out of business on 11 July 1960. Tranocean's Stratocruisers were bought up by Airline Equipment Inc., Newark, for just $105,000 and several were sold on to Lee Mansdorf and Aero Spacelines Inc.

Transocean Airlines Fleet

Con. no.	Model	Reg.	Notes
15927	377-10-26	N1027V	formerly G-ANUM (BOAC) later N401Q
15944	377-10-28	N103Q	formerly G-ALSB (BOAC) later N408Q did not enter service, to ASI
15945	377-10-28	N101Q	formerly G-ALSC (BOAC) later N406Q
15946	377-10-28	N85Q	formerly G-ALSD (BOAC) later N403Q
15965	377-20-29	N107Q	formerly G-ANTX (BOAC) later N412Q did not enter service, to ASI
15966	377-10-29	N108Q	formerly G-ANTY (BOAC) N413Q did not enter service, to ASI
15967	377-10-29	N106Q	formerly G-ANTZ (BOAC) N411Q did not enter service, to ASI
15968	377-10-29	N109A	formerly G-ANUA (BOAC) N414Q did not enter service, to ASI
15974	377-10-32	N137A	formerly G-AKGH (BOAC) later N402Q
15975	377-10-32	N100Q	formerly G-AKGI (BOAC) later N405Q to ASI
15976	377-10-32	N102Q	formerly G-AKGJ (BOAC) later N407Q to ASI
15977	377-10-32	N104Q	formerly G-AKGK (BOAC) later N409Q to ASI
15978	377-10-32	N86Q	formerly G-AKGL (BOAC) later N404Q to ASI
15979	377-10-32	N105Q	formerly G-AKGM (BOAC) later N410Q to ASI

LINEA INTERNACIONAL AEREA SA (LIA)

Based at Quito, this tiny Ecuadorian airline acquired a single ex-Pan American Stratocruiser in 1960 from Lee Mansdorf. The company had launched domestic services from Quito to Guayaquil in September 1958 and it hoped to use the Stratocruiser to extend that service to Miami. LIA won CAB approval to begin flights to the USA and the brightly-painted Stratocruiser was flown to Quito in December 1960. The registration HC-AGA was applied for the ferry flight, and marks HC-AFS were reserved for later use, but the aircraft never entered service. The Stratocruiser was seized by the Ecuadorian government and is believed to have been broken up some time after 1965 without ever flying again.

Lineas Internacional Aerea Fleet

Con. no.	Model	Reg.	Name	Notes
15940	Model-377-26	HC-AGA	*Princess Everetta Maria*	later HC-AFS formerly N1040V (PAA)

RUTAS AEREAS NACIONALES SA (RANSA)

The Venezuelan airline RANSA bought a total of ten former PAA Stratocruisers from Lee Mansdorf in 1961, which the aim of establishing freighter services to the US — chiefly Miami. RANSA started to convert the aircraft to an all-cargo configuration by adding a forward freight door on the starboard side. The first of its Stratocruiser freighters, (N1031V/YV-C-ERH) entered service on 5 October 1961 flying from Miami to Caracas. This aircraft was named in honour of the airline's chief pilot Carlos Nurse. RANSA's second aircraft, YV-C-ERI had the distinction of being the very first Stratocruiser — the prototype Model 377-10-19 (NX90700), it was later transferred to Pan American as a Model 377-10-26 (N1022V). This aircraft was named for the grand daughter of one of the senior pilots, Captain Chavez. RANSA placed three aircraft into service and was working on the conversion of a fourth (YV-C-ERK) when the airline went out of business on 6 September 1966. All four Stratocruisers in the RANSA fleet were impounded at Miami and were finally broken up there in 1969.

Rutas Aereas Nacionales SA Fleet

Con. No.	Model	Reg.	Name	Notes
15922	377-10-26	YV-C-ERI	*Carlos*	formerly N1022V (PAA), NX90700
15928	377-10-26	YV-C-ERJ	*Andreina Maria*	formerly N1028V (PAA)
15931	377-10-26	YV-C-ERH	*Princess Everetta Maria II*	formerly N1031V (PAA)
15934	377-10-26	YV-C-ERK		formerly N1034V (PAA)

ABOVE LEFT: Seen at Honolulu in 1959, Transocean's N409Q was formerly G-AKGK, a BOAC Model 377-10-32. Now fitted out with a high-density tourist-class cabin, this was the aircraft that once carried royalty for BOAC. *John Stroud Collection/Aviation Picture Library*

BELOW: YV-C-ERH was formerly *Clipper Mayflower* and then *Clipper Donald McKay* with Pan American. It had an eventful service career, which included a collision with an El Al Britannia at Idlewild in 1958. In RANSA hands she served for about five years between 1961 and 1966, when the company went out of business. *Stephen Piercey/Aviation Picture Library*

ISRAEL DEFENCE FORCE/AIR FORCE

Israel acquired five Stratocruisers and converted them to act as specialist military transports, alongside a larger number of C-97s, acquired later. Israel's Stratocruisers were the last active examples in the world and served from 1962 to 1975.

ISRAEL DEFENCE FORCE/AIR FORCE

Con. No.	Model	Reg.	Name	Notes
15925	377-10-26	4X-FOF	*Beitar*	4X-ASA later 4X-FPW/015 (with IAI) N1025V swing tail conversion
15930	377-10-26	4X-FOH	*Arbel*	4X-AOH later 4X-FPV/010 (with IAI) N1030V swing tail conversion
15962	377-10-29	4X-FOD	*Yodfat*	4X-AOG later 4X-FPZ (with IAI) N90946 clam-shell doors
15963	377-10-29	4X-FOG	*Zipori*	4X-AOD later 4X-FPX/098 (with IAI) N90947 clam-shell doors
15964	377-10-29	4X-FOI	*Massada*	4X-AOI later 4X-FPY/097 (with IAI) N90948 clam-shell doors

6 INCIDENTS AND ACCIDENTS

The Stratocruiser's Achilles heel proved to be its (Hamilton Standard) props and R-4360 Wasp Major engines. The Stratocruiser's entry into service was relatively trouble free, and it certainly did not suffer the same level of technical troubles that affected the Lockheed Constellation, the Douglas DC-6 or even the Avro Tudor. Engine reliability was the number one concern in those days, particularly on the long over-water flights, and many of the large four-engined transports vied for the dubious title of 'the best three-engined aircraft in the world'. Several Stratocruisers operators soon experienced problems with the aircraft's propeller design, and aircraft began to suffer dramatic in-flight prop losses. Prop failures would be implicated in several of the fatal Stratocruiser crashes that occurred in the years that followed. There would also be a series of in-flight engine stoppages.

The R-4360 was an immensely complicated piece of engineering that demanded constant maintenance of the highest order. With an airline like Pan American this is exactly what they received, but the R-4360 soon started to have a worrying effect on PAA's time keeping. On 7 July 1949 just five days after the launch of services to London, N1025V *Clipper America* made a three-engined diversion to Shannon Airport, after its port outer propeller sheered off some 800 miles (1,287km) out over the Atlantic. Snags with engine spark plugs and the turbosuperchargers forced two other aircraft to return to base the following month.

On 10 July an aircraft outbound from Tokyo was badly damaged when an engine suffered a catastrophic failure. Debris from the engine struck the fuselage and tail fin, forcing the Stratocruiser to make a rapid return. On 29 March 1951 Stratocruiser *Clipper United States* (N1032V) was on approach to Idlewild when parts of its number one propeller blade snapped off and the vibrations half-tore the engine out of its nacelle. This aircraft would later become the first of Pan American's Stratocruisers to crash.

United Air Lines also had an early run of bad luck. On 25 January 1950 Stratocruiser N74608 *Stratocruiser Tokyo* lost an entire engine off its wing, while the aircraft was flying from Minneapolis to New York. The emergency began when a section of the number one propeller broke off and sliced into the main cabin. No-one was hurt but while the aircraft was making an emergency descent into Glenview, Illinois, the number one engine then detached from the wing. The aircraft landed safely and a subsequent accident investigation found that the crew had taxyed the engine through a snow drift before take-off. However, the R-4360 and its complicated propellers had already shown a worrying propensity for failure and days after the United Air Lines incident the US authorities ordered an immediate safety inspection of all Stratocruiser propellers on a 'before next flight' basis. N74608 was involved in a second

incident, just a month later, on 28 February. While landing on a icy runway at Chicago the aircraft's props came into contact with the ground and were badly damaged. There were no injuries to any of the passengers or crew. This ill-starred aircraft suffered other serious incidents and would later become the only Northwest Stratocruiser to be lost in a crash.

THE FIRST FATALITIES

The first loss of life on a Stratocruiser occurred in tragic and unexpected circumstances. On 11 February 1950 a door blew out of a Pan American's *Clipper Mayflower* (N1031V) on approach to Idlewild while a steward, John Harris, was trying to secure it — Harris fell to his death. An almost identical incident occurred again, on 27 July 1952, on an outbound flight from Brazil (just three months after Pan American's first fatal crash, in Brazil). On this occasion a lady passenger was sucked out of a faulty door over the Atlantic, shortly after Stratocruiser *Clipper Southern Cross* (N1030V) had taken off from Rio. When the CAB investigated this incident it discovered that the crew had been warned that the door might be in an unsafe condition, but that the captain elected to continue the flight.

Clipper Mayflower, later *Clipper Donald McKay* (N1031V) had an eventful life. It flew the first New York–Shannon–London–Frankfurt service on 10 June 1949, but on 21 December 1949 it suffered a major in-flight emergency. The aircraft had a pressurisation failure and made an emergency descent from 23,000ft (7,010m) to land at Idlewild. In April 1958 N1031V collided with an El Al Britannia, while taxying at Idlewild.

On 3 January 1951 Pan American's Stratocruiser *Clipper Washington* (N1036V) was seriously damaged when it suffered an inadvertent gear retraction while landing at Heathrow. The aircraft was operating on an empty leg, following a weather diversion to Bournemouth the previous day, and had just nine crew aboard — none were injured. The pilot mistakenly selected 'right gear up' instead of the 'right flaps up', and the micro-switch safety system that was in place to prevent such a mishap only worked when the aircraft was on the ground with pressure on the undercarriage. Bizarrely, this same aircraft was damaged again in a similar incident when its crew failed to lower the undercarriage after a training flight on 30 May 1956.

Undercarriage troubles surfaced again, on 5 April 1950 when Stratocruiser *Clipper Morning Star* (N1042V) suffered a gear collapse during landing at San Francisco. The aircraft ground looped but there were no injuries to anyone on board.

In 1952 the first Stratocruiser was lost. This was a United Air Lines aircraft, *Mainliner Oahu* (N31230) while on a training flight. The three crew were all killed, but the aircraft was not carrying any passengers when it crashed into San Francisco Bay on 12 September 1951. The crash was finally attributed to pilot error and was another unfortunate, but explicable incident.

ABOVE: Though it experienced its fair-share of other mishaps and close calls, BOAC only lost one Stratocruiser over the years. On Christmas Day in 1954 G-ALSA *Cathay* crashed during a GCA approach to Prestwick Airport, killing the 24 passengers and four crew on board. At that point the Stratocruiser had amassed 9,704 hours of flight time since it entered service in December 1949. *via APL*

BOAC suffered its first accident on 24 April 1951. G-AKGL suffered a nosewheel collapse after a heavy landing at Prestwick, in Scotland. The nose section suffered severe damage, but none of the nine crew and 43 passengers on board were injured. The aircraft was returned to service after a complete rebuild from the nose section to the trailing edge of the wing.

THE FIRST LOSS

The first loss of a Stratocruiser on a passenger-carrying service came on 29 April 1952 when Pan American's N1039V *Clipper Good Hope* crashed in Brazil. The accident was caused by the separation of an engine and propeller while the aircraft was cruising and this became just the first such incident to claim a Stratocruiser and the lives of all on board.

On 6 December 1952 Pan American *Clipper Queen of the Pacific* (N90947) came close to disaster over the Pacific during a flight from San Francisco to Tokyo. About 700 miles (1,126km) out from Honolulu the Stratocruiser lost its number four propeller and engine in quick succession. The crew managed to retain control of the damaged aircraft and made an emergency landing at Johnson Atoll.

Three ditchings in the Pacific by Pan American World Airways aircraft followed, during 1955, 1956 and 1957, and these crashes did much to unnerve the Stratocruiser community. All three incidents involved a combination of propeller and engine failures. The 1957 crash was never fully explained as the aircraft disappeared with no distress calls ever received, some time after a routine position report had been made. The loss of this aircraft underlined how immature long-

range travel was, nearly ten years after the Stratocruiser had entered service.

Northwest Airlines had a good safety record and only ever suffered one fatal accident. This involved N74608 *Stratocruiser Tokyo* which crashed into Puget Sound after take-off from Seattle on 2 April 1956. All of the passengers and crew on board managed to escape from the aircraft but some drowned before the rescue teams could reach them. Apart from this incident Northwest's Stratocruisers suffered only minor incidents. The earlier loss of a propeller and an engine from N74608 on 25 January 1950 could have ended in disaster, but the crew managed to make a safe emergency landing.

On 5 August 1955 N74601 overran the runaway at Chicago-Midway Airport and crashed through the airport's boundary fence. One of the propellers had failed to select reverse pitch on landing and the aircraft could not be braked on time. None of the passengers were hurt but the aircraft was badly damaged. On 15 June 1957 Northwest's N74607 suffered a fire in its engine nacelle and wheel well on landing at Idlewild. A short while later another Northwest aircraft, N74603, was damaged in a hydraulics fire at Detroit on 28 July 1957.

Vying with Northwest's N74608 for the title of 'unluckiest Stratocruiser' was Pan American's N1035V. The *Clipper Flying Eagle* was involved in three separate serious incidents, all at New York, but never with any loss of life. On 10 May 1952 the Stratocruiser hit another aircraft while taxying at Idlewild. Two years later it was involved in a major drama when jammed nose-gear forced a gear-up landing on a foam covered runway on 6 March 1954. The aircraft had gear trouble yet again, on 12 December 1957, when its entire undercarriage caught fire after two aborted take-off attempts.

The last serious incident to involve an airline operated Stratocruiser came on 10 April 1959. On that date Pan American's *Clipper Midnight Sun* (N1033V) undershot while landing at Juneau, Alaska. The aircraft crashed and was destroyed by fire but all the passengers and crew escaped safely.

Date of incident: 12 September 1951
Aircraft registration: N31230
Airline: United Air Lines
Fatalities: three crew (of three on board)
Location: USA, San Francisco Bay

While operating crew training flight *United Trainer* 7030, the aircraft crashed into the Bay during a simulated ILS approach to San Francisco airport. The cause was attributed to an inadvertent stall at a low altitude. The aircraft had probably been flying with its number four engine feathered (simulating an emergency), the undercarriage had been lowered and the flaps were set down at 10°. It seems that with a high cockpit work load the crew simply allowed the aircraft to get away from them.

Date of incident: 29 April 1952
Airline: Pan American Airways
Aircraft registration: N1039V
Fatalities: all on board (nine crew, 41 passengers)
Location: Brazil, 400 miles (635 km) north-east of Barreiras
Flight Routing: PA202, Rio de Janeiro–New York

The aircraft departed Rio de Janeiro at 02.43hr for a direct (off airways) flight to Port-of-Spain, Trinidad. Last radio contact with the flight was at 06.16 when the crew reported at FL145 abeam Barreiras. The Stratocruiser crashed in dense jungle. The number two engine (inboard port) and propeller became unbalanced, then uncontrollable, and shook themselves loose from the aircraft. The cause was never fully established.

Date of incident: 25 December 1954
Airline: BOAC
Aircraft registration: G-ALSA
Fatalities: four crew, 24 passengers (of 11 and 25 on board)
Location: Prestwick, Scotland
Flight Routing: London–Prestwick

The Stratocruiser was high on its radar-controlled GCA approach to Prestwick. It entered a steep descent, but flared too late. Following a heavy landing, the plane ran onto the runway, became airborne again then crashed. The crash was attributed to errors of judgement on the part of the captain who started his final approach at too steep an angle and then flared out too late and too severely. As a result the aircraft sank and hit the ground short of the runway. Low cloud reduced the captain's visibility. The accident was also contributed to by the failure of the first officer to carry out an order to put on the landing lights, thus preventing the captain from seeing the low cloud over the approach lights in time. This same aircraft had only just been returned to service after suffering an undercarriage collapse while landing at Keflavik on 28 February 1954.

Date of incident: 26 March 1955
Airline: Pan American World Airways
Aircraft registration: N1032V
Fatalities: two crew and two passengers (of eight and 15 on board)

Location: USA, 35 miles off the coast of Oregon
Flight Routing: Portland–Honolulu

The number three (inboard starboard) engine and propelle tore loose from the wing, causing severe control difficultie The aircraft ditched, and sank after 20 minutes in the wate The cause of the accident was attributed to the loss of th engine and propeller and the resulting instability.

Date of incident: 2 April 1956
Airline: Northwest Airlines
Aircraft registration: N74608
Fatalities: one crew, four passengers (of six and 32 on board)
Location: 5.4 miles (8.7km) south-west of Seattle-Tacoma IAP, Washington
Flight Routing: Seattle-Tacoma–Portland

Northwest Flight 002 (Seattle–Portland–Chicago–New York took off from Seattle at 08.06hr. As the aircraft reached 2,000 (609m), at 145kt (166 mph/267km/h) airspeed, the flaps wer retracted. Suddenly, severe buffeting was experienced and th aircraft started to roll to the left. Assuming the aircraft was i asymmetric flap condition, the captain reduced power to sto the buffeting, but this had no effect. Full power was reapplie and plans were made to divert to McChord AFB, at Tacoma The plane continued to lose altitude, forcing a ditching i Puget Sound. The Stratocruiser sank 15 minutes later. Th crew executed a text-book ditching, with the captain and firs officer remaining on board to ensure that all the passengers ha escaped safely. Everyone was issued with lifejackets, but in th 35 minutes that it took for rescue boats to reach the acciden scene one member of the crew and four passengers drowned The aircraft was lifted from the sea bed and recovered for th crash investigation. It was soon determined that the aircraft ha taken off with its engine cowl flaps fully open and that none o the flight crew had noticed this serious failing in time.

Date of incident: 16 October 1956
Airline: Pan American World Airways
Aircraft registration: N90943
Fatalities: zero (of seven crew and 31 passengers on board)
Location: Pacific Ocean
Flight Routing: PA006, Honolulu–San Francisco

Clipper *Sovereign of the Skies* was on a round-the-world fligh from Philadelphia to San Francisco with stops in Europe, Asi and the Pacific. The aircraft took off from Honolulu a 20.26HST for the last leg of the flight to San Francisco. Th flight was cleared via Green Airway 9, track to 30°N, 140°W at FL130 and then at FL210 to San Francisco. At 01.02hr th crew requested a VFR climb to FL210, which was approved Immediately after reaching this altitude (at 01.19h) the numbe one (port outboard) engine oversped. The propeller could no be feathered, so the engine was frozen by cutting off its oi supply. As the aircraft was loosing altitude a ditching seeme inevitable. The US Coast Guard weather ship *November* wa

ABOVE: N1023V was renamed as *Clipper Golden Gate* after delivery, and became the fourth of the five Pan American Stratocruisers to be lost while in service. The aircraft crash landed in extreme weather at Manila, in June 1958. All but one of the 47 passengers on board survived the incident. *Boeing*

contacted at 01.22hr. Climb power was then applied to the remaining engines to try and reduce the rate of descent. The number four engine (outboard starboard) then began to only partially power at full throttle. The crew began to orbit November, waiting for daylight to carry out the ditching. At 02.45hr the number four engine finally failed but the prop was successfully feathered. At 05.40hr the captain contacted the Coast Guard vessel advising it of his ditching plan and began his slow descent. At 06.15hr the Stratocruiser was landed on the water. All the occupants were rescued and, 06.32hr the aircraft sank at position 30° 01.5'N, 140° 09'W.

Date of incident: 9 November 1957
Airline: Pan American World Airways
Aircraft registration: N90944
Fatalities: all on board (eight crew, 44 passengers)
Location: Pacific Ocean
Flight Routing: San Francisco–Honolulu

Clipper Romance of the Skies was operating a round-the-world flight from San Francisco, with its first stop at Honolulu. The aircraft departed San Francisco at 19.51hr GMT for the ten-hour first leg. The aircraft checked in with a routine position report at 01.04hr but after this nothing else was heard from the flight. A search was launched for the missing Stratocruiser and, on 14 November, the US Navy carrier USS *Philippine Sea* located bodies and parts of wreckage some 940 miles (1,512km) east of Honolulu and 90 miles (145km) north of the intended track. Insufficient wreckage was recovered to allow crash investigators to find a cause for the crash.

Date of incident: 2 June 1958
Airline: Pan American World Airways
Aircraft registration: N1023V
Fatalities: no crew, one passenger (of eight and 49 on board)
Location: Manila, the Philippines
Flight Routing: San Francisco– Singapore

The Stratocruiser was *en route* San Francisco–Singapore with the usual intermediary fuel stops. As the aircraft touched down at Manila its undercarriage collapsed. The weather was bad with a strong crosswind and in a heavy landing the right main gear 'V' strut failed. The Stratocruiser skidded and swerved to the right, coming to rest 2,850ft (868.6m) past the runway threshold and 27ft (8.2m) from the edge of the runway. One passenger was killed when the blades of the number three prop broke off and cut into the main cabin.

Date of incident: 9 July 1959
Airline: Pan American World Airways
Aircraft registration: N90941
Fatalities: none (six crew and 53 passengers on board)
Location: Tokyo, Japan
Flight Routing: to Tokyo

The *Clipper Australia* was approaching Tokyo when the undercarriage was extended. The gear indicator showed 'three greens', signifying that the gear was down and locked. When power was reduced prior to touchdown, the gear unsafe warning horn sounded and a warning light lit up. The captain called for a go-around, but airspeed was too low. The gear was quickly retracted and a safe belly landing was made.

Date of incident: August 1967
Airline: Aero Spacelines Inc.
Aircraft registration: N90942
Fatalities: none
Location: Mojave, California

While preparing for a ferry flight to Santa Barbara the aircraft was badly damaged in a ground collision with Stratocruiser N402Q.

The incredible Guppies were the creation of Jack Conroy and Lee Mansdorf. Mansdorf had bought up many of the unwanted Stratoliners that came on the market from 1960 onwards. He had an available resource of aircraft, but little demand for them. Conroy had the aeronautical engineering background to see that the Stratocruisers might be the perfect basis to produce an outsize freighter. In 1961 Conroy founded Aero Spacelines Inc. NASA was immersed in the space race and was building bigger and better rockets in its efforts to beat the Russians in the manned space programme. However, the bigger the rockets got the more difficult it was to transport them to where they needed to be, and so Conroy and Mansdorf hit upon the idea of the Guppy to get them there. The unflattering Guppy name — a guppy is a big, fat fish — was applied more in jest than anything else, but it stuck. When the aircraft, developed an rebuilt specially by Aero Spacelines Inc., proved to be a grea success the Guppy name became a proud one. The Guppie were the only way to move outsized loads quickly, and fo decades they remained totally unique aircraft. Despite their ag and their ever increasing cost of operations, they were absolutel irreplaceable. The last major user of the type was Airbu Industrie, which flew four turboprop-powered Super Gupp 201s on regular routes around Europe picking up and deliverin sub-assemblies for Airbus airliners. When Airbus was forcec finally, to replace its Super Guppies it had to build a whole ne class of air transport. Remarkably, one of the Airbus aircra returned to its spiritual homeland and is still flying today, i the hands of NASA in the United States.

BELOW: The four Super Guppies operated by Airbus Industrie were an integral part of the European planemaker's operation. For many years, they ferried major sub-assemblies built by the Airbus partners in the UK, Spain and Germany to the final assembly site at Toulouse, in the south of France. *Airbus*

RIGHT: The Airbus Super Guppy 201s were flown by the French airline Aéromaritime on behalf of the consortium. Aéromaritime was, in turn, an operating subsidiary of UTA, which had assembled two additional aircraft for Airbus in 1982/83 in conjunction with Tracor Aviation. *Airbus*

MODEL B377PG PREGNANT GUPPY
N1024V, N126AJ

The Pregnant Guppy, as it became known, was the first of the Guppy conversions and it was built to carry the 40ft (12.19m) long and 18ft (5.48m) wide stages of the Saturn IV moon rocket. Aero Spacelines used the fuselage of Stratocruiser c/n 15924 as its main 'airframe of reference' for the Model 377PG. This was the second production Model 377 and was delivered to Pan American as N1024V. It was traded back Boeing, as part of the PAA 707 deal, in 1961. Boeing sold the aircraft to Lee Mansdorf, who in turn sold it to ASI. A second Model 377 was also involved in the construction of the 377PG. This was aircraft 15976, the former G-AKGJ of BOAC, which later became N407Q with Transocean. This aircraft was also brokered by Lee Mansdorf to ASI.

ABOVE: The Pregnant Guppy conversion, undertaken by On Mark Engineering together with Aero Spacelines, was a remarkable achievement – but it was not yet perfect. Because the entire tail section had to detached to load the aircraft, this process could be an overly-difficult and time-consuming one. *via Kenneth Gibson*

BELOW: The Pregnant Guppy's first job was to carry the Douglas-built S-4 second stage of the Saturn 1 launch vehicle, the associated Rocketdyne F-1 engine and other NASA cargo. Later the B377PG carried the larger S-4 stage, around which i had been originally designed. *Boeing*

To build the Pregnant Guppy a section of fuselage measurin 16ft 8in (5.12m) was added to the base aircraft, aft of the wing trailing edge. The upper fuselage was expanded to 19ft (5.79m allowing a little clearance for the rocket sections. The Pregnan Guppy was not a true swing-tail conversion, indeed its entir tail section had to be detached for loading. The B377PC measured 127ft (38.7m) long with a wingspan of 141ft 3in (43m

this much revised form the Pregnant Guppy made its maiden flight on 19 September 1962 with Jack Conroy and Clay Lacy at the controls. The aircraft was flown to NASA's Marshall Space Flight Center, at Huntsville, Alabama — where the director of the Center, the former-Nazi rocket scientist Werner Von Braun, became one of the first passengers to fly in Guppy. Soon after this the Pregnant Guppy name was first coined and Aero Spacelines got the 'OK' from NASA to proceed with the final structural work it required. In all, the conversion was costed at approximately $1 million.

The Pregnant Guppy weighed in at a massive 91,000lb (41,278kg), but only 3,000lb (1,361kg) more than a Stratoliner. While the 377PG was big, it had none of the interior systems and cabin fittings that a passenger airliner demanded. It had a maximum cruise speed of 250mph (402km/h) with a 29,000lb (13,154kg) payload. The original R-4360 piston engines were retained. The 377PG used its own dedicated loading system, the Cargo Lift Trailer (CLT) and needed a special support system to remove the tail section.

Between 1962 and 1963 the Pregnant Guppy underwent flight tests at Edwards AFB. NASA was becoming increasingly eager to get the aircraft into service, as it would cut the transportation time for a Saturn rocket section from up to 25 days to about 18 hours. The Pregnant Guppy was certified as a public aircraft (that is, outside normal FAA regulations) on 10 July 1963. The Model 377PG remained in service for 17 years and during that time its ownership passed to American Jet Industries, in 1974 (as N126AJ). The single Pregnant Guppy was dismantled in 1979 and its lower aft fuselage was used in the construction of the fourth Super Guppy 201 for Airbus.

MODEL B377SG SUPER GUPPY
N1038V, N940NA, N940NS

The success of the Model 377PG prompted Aero Spacelines to build a bigger, better Guppy — the Very Pregnant Guppy or, as it later became known, the Super Guppy. The first Model 377SG flew on 31 August 1965 and it too played an integral role in the US space programme. The Super Guppy was intended to cruise faster than the Pregnant Guppy (up to 265mph/426km/h) with a heavier payload (40,000lb/18,144kg). ASI took a former Pan American Stratocruiser (N1038V, c/n 15938) and used major sections from the two ex-USAF YC-97J engine testbeds to produce the first Super Guppy. NASA made a direct application to the Air Force to make the two YC-97Js available for the conversion, allowing it to go ahead as quickly as possible. The Super Guppy retained the Pratt & Whitney T-34P9W engines that had been fitted to the YC-97Js — making it the first turboprop-powered Guppy.

BELOW: Closely followed by a Learjet 23 chase plane, this photo may well have been taken during the Super Guppy's first flight, in August 1965. The Super Guppy (or the 'VPG' as it was initially known) was able to carry the Douglas S-IVB third stage of the Saturn V moon rocket. *via Kenneth Gibson*

The Super Guppy conversion was very different to the Pregnant Guppy, For a start it was a front-loader with a swing-nose. It was also fully pressurised. The fuselage was stretched using two 'plugs' — an 18ft (5.48m) forward section and an 8ft (2.43m) section aft. The diameter of the main cargo cabin was increased to 25ft (7.62m) and all the tail surfaces were enlarged. The aircraft measured 141ft 3in (43m) in length and had a wingspan of 156ft 3in (47.64m).

The Super Guppy made its maiden flight from Van Nuys Airport, California. Due to a particular aerodynamic quirk the Super Guppy's rear main gear usually left the ground before the nose wheels, leading to a most unusual take-off run. Le[ss] than a month into the fight test programme the Super Gup[py] experienced an in-flight structural failure, on 25 Septemb[er] 1965. A section of the upper forward fuselage blew out, but t[he] aircraft was able to land safely and was soon repaired.

NASA was in a hurry to get the Super Guppy into servi[ce] as soon as possible and by March 1966 the aircraft was carryi[ng] loads for the space programme. The Super Guppy continued [to] carry outsize loads for a variety of customers throughout t[he] 1960s and 1970s. It was bought by NASA in 1979 and r[e-] registered as N940NA.

MODEL B377MG MINI-GUPPY
N1037V, N422AU

The Mini-Guppy was the third Guppy conversion and, with the experience of the first two aircraft to draw on, Aero Spacelines approached the conversion in a more 'productionised' way. The baseline 'aircraft of reference' was c/n 15937, the one-time N1037V with Pan American. ASI acquired it, through Lee Mansdorf, in 1963.

Despite its name, there was nothing small about the Mini-Guppy. ASI designed an entirely new fuselage to join two existing Stratocruiser nose and tail sections. This did away with the 8ft (2.43m) floor width restriction of the Pregnant Guppy and the Super Guppy. Instead, ASI built the first wide-bodied Guppy. It's cargo hold floor measured 13ft (3.96m) across, while its maximum diameter was 18ft (5.48m). Thanks to the new main fuselage insert the Mini-Guppy had a constant-section cargo hold that was about 73ft (22.25m) long. The

ABOVE: The Mini-Guppy became the first of the Guppies to be fully FAA-certifie[d] — the earlier aircraft had operated under special government service rules. FAA approval was required in order for Aero Spacelines to undertake commercial hire work, chiefly carrying DC-10 and L-1011 sub-assemblies. *via Kenneth Gibson*

Mini-Guppy weighed in at 85,000lb (38,556kg), empty, an[d] had a maximum payload of 41,120lb (18,652kg). It was th[e] shortest of the Guppy conversions, measuring 132ft 10i[n] (40.47m) in length with a wingspan of 156ft 3in (47.64m). Th[e] Mini-Guppy was a swing-tail conversion, that did away wit[h] the removable tail arrangement of the Model 377PG.

Named *The Spirit of Santa Barbara* the Mini-Guppy mad[e] its first flight on 24 May 1967. Two days later it made its firs[t] revenue-earning flight, carrying exhibition material to the Par[is] Air Show. While in France the Mini-Guppy was demonstrate[d] to Aerospatiale, which was already wondering how to solve th[e] questions surrounding component transport for the nascen[t]

pan-European Airbus project. However, like its sisterships, the Mini-Guppy became a solution in search of a problem and operators found it difficult to keep the aircraft gainfully employed. The Mini-Guppy had a succession of owners, passing from Aero Spacelines to American Jet Industries, in 1974, then to Aero Union, in 1980, and then to Erickson Air

ABOVE: Aero Spacelines once proposed an 'auto air ferry' version of the Mini-Guppy, with drive-on ramps leading to two decks inside the main fuselage, and passengers carried in a third lower deck. *via Kenneth Gibson*

BELOW: This is how the Mini-Guppy appeared during its days with Aero-Union. When a British Airways Helicopters Chinook crashed into the North Sea in 1984, the Mini-Guppy came to Aberdeen to fly the remains back to Boeing, in February the following year. *via Kenneth Gibson*

Crane, in 1988. It was the Mini-Guppy that was actually the star of the 1992 film *Universal Soldier*, when it hove into view during the film's sweeping opening sequence — and made an impressive side-slip landing. In 1995 the aircraft was finally retired to the Erickson College of Aeronautics, at the Tillamook Naval Air Station Museum.

MODEL 377MGT MINI-GUPPY TURBINE
(GUPPY 101)
s/n 0001   N111AS (N4020)

One of the most important factors holding back the early Guppy conversions was the retention of their original R-4360 Wasp Major piston engines. These were increasingly difficult to support and costly to maintain, so Aero Spacelines began to look around for a more modern alternative.

The MGT used essentially the same airframe as the Mini-Guppy, but fitted it with four Allison 501-D22C turboprops, each rated at 4,680shp (3,491kW). The 501 engine was a civil version of the T-56 powerplant used by the Lockheed P-3

Orion, and ASI even adopted the Orion's entire engine nacelle design to speed things up. The Hamilton Standard 54H60 propellers and spinners were taken from the C-130. The MGT had an empty weight of 90,000lb (40,823kg) and a maximum payload of 62,925lb (28,542kg). The aircraft was based on C-97 airframes and measured 135ft 6in (41.30m) in length with a wingspan of 156ft 3in (47.64m).

The Mini-Guppy Turbine made its maiden flight on 13 March 1970, from ASI's facility at Santa Barbara Airport, California. With the MGT, Aero Spacelines at last had a truly commercial aircraft with which to go looking for business. Unfortunately, the sole example crashed during flight testing at Edwards AFB on 12 May 1970.

MODEL 377SGT SUPER GUPPY TURBINE
(GUPPY 201)
s/n 0001   N211AS, F-BTGV *Airbus Skylink 1*
s/n 0002   N212AS, F-BPPA *Airbus Skylink 2*
s/n 0003   F-GDSG *Airbus Skylink 3*
s/n 0004   F-GEAD *Airbus Skylink 4,* **N941NA**

With the last and most successful of the Guppy conversions Aero Spacelines returned to the original Super Guppy hull-form and added new Allison 501-D22C turboprops. These were the same engines that had been fitted to the ill-fated Mini-Guppy Turbine. Though it looked similar, the shape of the main fuselage was different to that of the original Super Guppy thanks to ASI's more refined production techniques. The SGT

ABOVE: This artist's impression of the Super Guppy Turbine was not too wide of the mark. It is certainly less fanciful than some of the Aero Spacelines proposals, such as a six-engined Super Guppy and the astonishing Colossal Guppy based on a B-52 fuselage with a 40ft (12.2m) diameter fuselage. *Aero Spacelines*

used very few original parts — all taken from C-97s — and had a purpose-built main fuselage. Inside, the SGT had a roller cargo handling system, allowing loads to be moved around the aircraft before being locked into place. The SGT was the largest of the Guppies, with an available cargo volume of 39,000cu ft (1,104m³). It had a fuselage diameter of 25ft (7.62m) with a 13ft (3.96m) wide floor. The cargo hold offered a single constant section of 25ft (7.62m) x 32ft (9.75m). It was a swing-nose Guppy, that used a special powered loading dolly once in Airbus service. The Super Guppy Turbine weighed 99,500lb

(45,133kg) empty, and had a maximum payload of 54,500lb (24,721kg). It was 143ft 10in (43.8m) long and had a wingspan of 156ft 3in (47.64m).

ASI had intended to operate the SGT in its own right, but the company was suffering from serious financial troubles. Airbus, meanwhile, had not forgotten its earlier brush with the Guppy and contracted to buy one SGT in 1970. The first SGT, N211AS, made its maiden flight on 24 August 1970. This aircraft was sold to Airbus, who ordered a second aircraft to be

ABOVE: Airbus took delivery of its first Super Guppy 201 ('Airbus Skylink 1', F-BTGV) in November 1971. Once that aircraft had been certified, work began in ernest on the second aircraft (F-BPPA), which entered service in August 1973. Two additional aircraft were acquired in the early 1980s. Tracor (which had by then bought out Aero spacelines in 1981) provided the empennage, nose and wings. UTA Industries built the additional fuselage section and undertook final assembly. This is the last of the SGTs, 'Skylink 4'. *British Aerospace*

BELOW: A fuselage section from the second Airbus A300 is loaded onto a Super Guppy 201 at Aerospatiale's Saint-Nazaire factory, for delivery to Toulouse. Note the purpose-built trolley/loader. *Airbus*

ABOVE AND BELOW: Not only Airbuses got to fly by Super Guppy. In January 1980 Aéromaritime was contracted by British Aerospace to fly BAC One-Eleven fuselage sections from Filton to Bucharest, as part of the ROMBAC One-Eleven programme. Until 1991 the Super Guppies were a regular sight at Filton (home of British Aerospace Airbus) where they would call to ferry out A320 wing sections. That year the task of wing transportation was moved from air to road, as the Guppies concentrated on hauling larger Airbus sub-assemblies. The road journey from Bristol to Toulouse took five days. *British Aerospace*

ABOVE: The last Super Guppy 201 was retired by Airbus in 1997, but this aircraft — the youngest of all the Guppies — still remains in active service. It was acquired by NASA and is in operation today, once again hauling out-size cargo for the space programme. *Airbus*

available as a back-up. The second SGT, N212AS, flew on 24 August 1972 and this was acquired by Airbus in 1973. Airbus Industrie's production rates increased to such a level that within a few years it needed to double its Super Guppy Turbine fleet, and so ordered two more in 1978/79. Sub-assemblies for these aircraft were delivered in 1978 and 1979, and the finished Guppies flew in 1979 and 1980. A second pair of Super Guppy 201s were built in France, by UTA, these were designated as Model 377SGT-Fs.

Aero Spacelines' money troubles eventually became too much for the company and it was sold to Tracor Inc., which became Tracor Aviation in 1981. Tracor was then sold to Lucas Aerospace, becoming Lucas Aviation and it was this company that provided support for the Airbus SGTs until the end of their operational careers. In 1996 SGT No. 1 was retired and

bought by the British Aviation Heritage Trust, at Bruntingthorpe, where the aircraft is stored today. SGT No. 2 was also withdrawn in 1996 and is preserved at Airbus headquarters, in Toulouse, where it forms part of the wider Ailes Anciennes historic collection. In late 1997 SGT No. 3 was retired by Deutsche Airbus facility, in Hamburg. However, SGT No. 4 is still active. After its withdrawal by Airbus it was re-registered as N941NA and taken on charge by NASA. The SGT was delivered to Ellington Field, Houston, on 23 October 1997 and now operates from the Johnson Space Center. It is being used to carry outside loads for the International Space Station programme and other NASA activities.

Aero Spacelines Inc. acquired a total of 27 Model 377s and Model 367s for use in the Guppy programme. The aircraft were stored largely at ASI's base in Mojave, Arizona, though some went to Oakland, California. All were ultimately scrapped. Major assemblies or sizeable numbers of part were taken from the following Stratocruisers:

CON. NO.	PREVIOUS IDENTITIES	NOTES
15924	N1024V	Model 377PG, parts to Model 377SG No. 4
15938	N1038V	Model 377SG Super Guppy
15944	G-ALSB, N103Q, N408Q	Model 377SG
15945	G-ALSC, N101Q, N406Q	Model 377SG
15947	N74601	crashed in August 1995 but used in Model 377MG
15967	N31227, G-ANTZ, N106Q, N211Q	Model 377MG
15976	G-AKGJ, N102Q, N407Q	Model 377PG
15934	N1034V, (YV-C-ERK)	ASI cargo conversion?
15949	N74603	acquired 1963. Used (unmodified) for publicity purposes
15952	N74606	acquired 1963. Fitted with side cargo door, scrapped

8 PRODUCTION HISTORY

Between July 1947 and December 1949 Boeing built a total of 56 Stratocruisers. Just as it does today, Boeing attached specific customer numbers to those aircraft.

Model 377-10-19: Boeing Airplane Company. Prototype only (later to Pan American as 377-10-26).

Model 377-10-26: PAA, Pan American World Airways. 20 aircraft ordered. Circular windows.

Model 377-10-27: intended order for ten from Transcontinental & Western Air Lines (TWA). Not built.

Model 377-10-28: SILA (Svensk Interkontinental Luftrafik). Four ordered but not delivered, aircraft to BOAC instead Circular windows.

Model 377-10-29: AOA, American Overseas Airways. Eight aircraft ordered. Circular windows on main deck, rectangular below.

Model 377-10-30: NWA, Northwest Airlines (later Northwest Orient Airlines). Ten aircraft ordered. Rectangular windows.

Model 377-10-32: BOAC, British Overseas Airways Corporation. Six aircraft ordered. Circular windows with none aft of wing on port side.

Model 377-10-34: UAL, United Air Lines. Seven aircraft ordered. Rectangular windows on main deck, circular below.

BOEING MODEL 377
STRATOCRUISER PRODUCTION LIST

LINE NUMBER: 15922   **MODEL 377-10-19/26**
Roll-out: 2 July 1947   **First flight:** 8 July 1947   **Delivered:** 24 October 1950
NX90700: prototype. Delivered as N1022V
N1022V: redelivered to Pan American as *Clipper Nightingale*, and rebuilt as a Model 377-10-26. Withdrawn and stored at Miami, 1960. Sold to Lee Mansdorf, then to RANSA
YV-C-ERI: RANSA, 1961. Converted to freighter with forward cargo door 1961. Named *Carlos* for chief pilot Carlos Nurse. Repossessed after bankruptcy. Broken up, Miami, July 1969

LINE NUMBER: 15923   **MODEL 377-10-26**
Roll-out: 15 March 1948   **First flight:** 17 April 1948   **Delivered:** 19 March 1949
N1023V: Pan American *Clipper America*, later *Clipper Golden Gate*. Written off after heavy landing in Manila, 2 June 1958. Airframe dismantled

LINE NUMBER: 15924   **MODEL 377-10-26**
Roll-out: 8 April 1948   **First flight:** 7 October 1948   **Delivered:** 12 June 1949
NX1024V: retained by Boeing for flight tests
N1024V: Pan American *Clipper Bald Eagle* later *Clipper Cathay*. Withdrawn and stored, Miami, 1960. Traded back to Boeing in January 1961. Sold to Lee Mansdorf, then Aero Spacelines. Converted to Pregnant Guppy configuration, 1962
N126AJ: sold by ASI to American Jet Industries, later broken up for spares

LINE NUMBER 15925   **MODEL 377-10-26**
Roll-out: 8 October 1948   **First flight** 4 December 1948   **Delivered:** 31 January 1949
N1025V: Pan American *Clipper America*, later *Clipper Rainbow*, *Clipper Celestial*. Withdrawn in 1961. Sold to Israeli Aircraft Industries in February 1962
4X-AOF: delivered to Israel on 25 April 1962
4X-ASA: re-registered for conversion work by IAI, 1962. Converted to swing-tail freighter by IAI at Lod
4X-FPW/015: new registration and serial allocated on return to IDF service, 1 June 1965. Struck off 1 December 1975

LINE NUMBER: 15926   **MODEL 377-10-26**
Roll-out: 3 December 1948   **First flight:** 1 February 1949   **Delivered:** 17 February 1949
N1026V: Pan American *Clipper Trade Wind*, later *Clipper Malay*. Traded in to Boeing on 2 July 1961, then to Lee Mansdorf. Sold to RANSA 1961. Never converted to freighter, broken up Miami, February 1969

ABOVE: NX90700, the prototype Model 377-10- 19 Stratocruiser, ground-running on a spot-lit Renton ramp. *Boeing*

LINE NUMBER: 15927   **MODEL 377-10-26**
Roll-out: 17 December 1948   **First flight:** 12 February 1949   **Delivered:** 2 March 1949
N1027V: Pan American *Clipper Friendship*. Sold to BOAC 26 August 1954
G-ANUM: BOAC RMA *Clyde*. Configured with 81-seat 'Coronet' seating. Served with West African Airways until March 1958. Sold to TAL, via the Babb Company, on 7 July 1958
N1027V: Transocean Air Lines. Converted to 40-seat layout
N401Q: Transocean re-registered June 1958. Sold at auction to Airline Equipment Company 1 September 1960, sold via Mansdorf to ASI. Broken up for spares

ABOVE: N1023V *Clipper America*, Pan American Airway's first Model 377-10-16 Stratocruiser. *Boeing*

ABOVE: N1030V *Clipper Southern Cross* later became 4X-FPV and was converted to a swing-tail freighter by the Israeli Air Force. *Boeing*

LINE NUMBER:15928   **MODEL 377-10-26**
Roll-out: 14 January 1949   **First flight:** 18 February 1949   **Delivered:** 14 March 1949
N1028V: Pan American *Clipper Flying Cloud*. Traded in to Boeing 7 February 1961. Sold to Mansdorf then to RANSA
YV-C-ERJ: RANSA *Andreina Maria* April 1961, freighter conversion July 1961. Repossessed in September 1966 and later broken up, Miami, 30 April 1969

LINE NUMBER:15929   **MODEL 377-10-26**
Roll-out: 22 March   **First flight:** 2 April 1949   **Delivered:** 22 April 1949
N1029V: Pan American *Clipper Golden Eagle*. Badly damaged in gear-up landing at Heathrow on 30 April 1952. Converted to Super Stratocruiser. Stored 1960 and returned to Boeing 7 February 1961. Sold via Mansdorf to RANSA, re-registered to Miami Air Charters July 1966. Never entered service. Broken up, Miami, April 1968. Parts to IAI

LINE NUMBER:15930   **MODEL 377-10-26**
Roll-out: 11 February 1949   **First flight:** 11 March 1949   **Delivered:** 30 March 1949
N1030V: Pan American *Clipper Southern Cross*, later *Clipper Reindeer*, *Clipper America*. Chartered by US Navy for operations to McMurdo Sound during Operation 'Deep Freeze III', 1957. Withdrawn and stored 1960, sold to IAI 2 February 1962
4X-AOH: IAI February 1962. Delivered by May 1962
4X-FOH: IDF/AF, November 1962. Converted to swingtail freighter by IAI at Lod
4X-FPV/010: new registration and serial allocated on return to IDF service 16 May 1965. Withdrawn and broken up for spares September 1972, Tel Aviv

LINE NUMBER: 15931   **MODEL 377-10-26**
Roll-out: 1 April 1949   **First flight:** 17 April 1949   **Delivered:** 28 March 1949
N1031V: Pan American *Clipper Mayflower*, later *Clipper Donald McKay*. Withdrawn and stored 1960, traded to Boeing 7 February 1961. Sold to Ransdorf, then RANSA. US marks retained initially
YV-C-ERH: RANSA fitted with forward cargo door, September 1961. Flew first service 5 October 1961. Withdrawn 1966 and broken up, July 1969, Miami

LINE NUMBER: 15932   **MODEL 377-10-26**
Roll-out: 19 April 1949   **First flight:** 30 April 1949   **Delivered:** 22 May 1949
N1032V: Pan American *Clipper United States*. Ditched into the Pacific, off north-west coast of USA, 26 March 1955

ABOVE: N1035V *Clipper Flying Eagle*, a Pan American Model 377-10-26, poses over Windsor Castle. *via William Doyle*

LINE NUMBER: 15933   **MODEL 377-10-26**
Roll-out: 13 May 1949   **First flight::** 22 May 1949   **Delivered:** 22 June 1949
N1033V: Pan American *Clipper Seven Seas*, later *Clipper Midnight Sun* (when re-assigned to Alaskan services). Crashed on landing and destroyed by fire, Juneau, Alaska, 10 April 1959.

LINE NUMBER: 15934   **MODEL 377-10-26**
Roll-out: 20 May 1949   **First flight:** 6 March 1949   **Delivered:** 3 July 1949
N1034V: Pan American *Clipper Westward Ho*. Withdrawn and stored Miami, October 1961. To RANSA
YV-C-ERK: RANSA, but marks not taken up. In preparation for cargo conversion when airline went out of business. Sold to MAC
N1034V: reverted to original identity with Miami Air Charters. Stored and broken up, Miami, May 1969

LINE NUMBER: 15935   **MODEL 377-10-26**
Roll-out: 26 April 1949   **First flight:** 9 June 1949   **Delivered:** 23 July 1949
N1035V: Pan American *Clipper Flying Eagle*. Returned to Boeing 2 July 1961, sold to Mansdorf then RANSA. Not registered to RANSA, passed to Miami Air Charters. Stored and broken up, Miami, May 1968

LINE NUMBER: 15936   **MODEL 377-10-26**
Roll-out: 30 June 1949   **First flight:** 20 July 1949   **Delivered:** 12 August 1949
N1036V: Pan American *Clipper Washington*. Sold to Alfred Equipment Company, then to RANSA. Intended to become YV-C-ERL but marks not taken up. Stored and broken up, Miami, February 1968. Parts to IAI

ABOVE: Stratocruiser NX1039V was a Pan American aircraft (*Clipper Good Hope*) used by Boeing for initial test and trials flying. *Boeing*

LINE NUMBER: 15937   **MODEL 377-10-26**
Roll-out: 13 July 1949   **First flight:** 11 August 1949   **Delivered:** 8 September 1949
N1037V: Pan American *Clipper Fleetwing*. Sold to Aero Spacelines, 1963. Converted to B377-MG Mini-Guppy *Spirit of Santa Barbar*a. First flew 24 May 1967. Sold to AJI
N422AJ: American Jet Industries
N422AU: Aero Union, July 1981, then Erickson Air Crane. Retired, and preserved at Tilamook

LINE NUMBER: 15938   **MODEL 377-10-26**
Roll-out: 22 July 1949   **First flight:** 20 August 1949   **Delivered:** 29 September 1949
N1038V: Pan American *Clipper Constitution*, later *Clipper Hotspur*. Retired and stored, Idlewild, sold to Boeing 4 August 1960. Sold to Mansdorf, then to Aero Spacelines Inc. Converted to B377-SG Super Guppy configuration using components from 15944 and 15945. First flight 31 August 1965. Sold to NASA 1979.
N940NA, later . . .
N940NS: NASA. Withdrawn from use 1995, into storage at the Pima County Museum

LINE NUMBER: 15939   **MODEL 377-10-26**
Roll-out: 17 September 1947   **First flight:** 28 September 1949   **Delivered:** 27 August 1949
NX1039V: Retained by Boeing for the flight test programme before delivery
N1039V: Pan American *Clipper Good Hope*. Crashed in Brazilian jungle, near Carolina, 29 April 1952

LINE NUMBER: 15940   **MODEL 377-10-26**
Roll-out: 1 September 1949   **First flight:** 23 September 1949   **Delivery** 31 October 1949
N1040V: Pan American *Clipper Invincible*. Withdrawn, stored at Idlewild and returned to Boeing 4 August 1960. Sold to Mansdorf, then to LIA.
HC-AGA then . . .
HC-AFS: Linea Internacional Aereo, SA *Princess Everetta Maria*, 1960. Allocated dual registration for ferry flight/service. Wfu, stored and broken up Quito, Ecuador late-1965/66

LINE NUMBER: 15941   **MODEL 377-10-26**
Roll-out: 9 September 1949   **First flight:** 5 October 1949   **Delivered:** 8 November 1949
N1041V: Pan American *Clipper Yankee*, later *Clipper Northern Light*. Withdrawn, stored at Idlewild then sold to Alfred Equipment Company 25 October 1961. Ferried to Miami, registered to Aero Central 1 July 1964. Scrapped May 1966, parts to RANSA and IAI

ABOVE: G-ALSC *Centaurus*, a Model 377-10-28 was the third aircraft to be delivered to BOAC. It was ultimately broken up for spares by Aero Spacelines. *via William Doyle*

LINE NUMBER: 15942   **MODEL 377-10-26**
Roll-out: 11 November 1949   **First flight:** 5 December 1949   **Delivered:** 30 December 1949
N1042V: Pan American *Clipper Morning Star*, later *Clipper Polynesi*a. Withdrawn, stored at Miami and returned to Boeing 25 January 1961. Sold to Lee Mansdorf, then to Aero Spacelines, 1963. Stored Mojave, then broken up 1963

LINE NUMBER: 15943   **MODEL 377-10-28**
Roll-out: 1 July 1949   **First flight:** 6 July 1949   **Delivered:** 12 October 1949
SE-BDP: SILA, marks not taken up, sold to BOAC
G-ALSA: BOAC, RMA *Cathay*. Crashed, Prestwick, 25 December 1954

LINE NUMBER: 15944   **MODEL 377-10-28**
Roll-out: 18 August 1949   **First flight:** 16 September 1949   **Delivered:** 24 October 1949
OY-DFY: SILA, marks not taken up, sold to BOAC
G-ALSB: BOAC RMA *Champion*. Sold to the Babb Company and delivered to Transocean 3 February 1959.
N103Q: Transocean Air Lines marks not taken up. Re-registered
N408Q: TAL, did not enter service. Sold to Airline Equipment Inc., 1 September 1960, then to ASI, 1963. Used in conversion of B377SG Super Guppy N1038V

LINE NUMBER: 15945   **MODEL 377-10-28**
Roll-out: 20 September 1949   **First flight:** 28 October 1949   **Delivered:** 2 December 1949
LN-LAF: SILA, marks not taken up, sold to BOAC
G-ALSC: BOAC, RMA *Centaurus*. Retired 5 January 1959. Sold to the Babb Company, then to TAL
N101Q: Trans Ocean Air Lines, registered 8 January 1959.
N406Q: re-registered 14 October 1959. Sold to Airline Equipment Inc., 1 September 1960, then to ASI via Mansdorf, 1963. Used in conversion of B377SG Super Guppy N1038V

LINE NUMBER: 15946   **MODEL 377-10-28**
Roll-out: 19 October 1949   **First flight:** 9 November 1949   **Delivered:** 16 December 1949
SE-BDR: SILA, marks not taken up, sold to BOAC
G-ALSD: BOAC, RMA *Cassiopeia*. Retired and sold via the Babb Company to TAL, delivered 7 September 1958
N85Q: Transocean Air Lines
N403Q: re-registered 1959. Sold to Airline Equipment Inc., 1 September 1960, then to ASI via Mansdorf, 1963. Broken up for parts

ABOVE: N74601 *Stratocruiser Manila*, was the first Model 377-10-30 to be delivered to Northwest Airlines. In 1967 it was finally broken up for spares at Santa Barbara. *Boeing*

LINE NUMBER: 15947   **MODEL 377-10-30**
Roll-out: 18 February 1949   **First flight:** 18 March 1949   **Delivered:** 29 July 1949
N74601: Northwest Airlines, *Stratocruiser Manila*. Retired and traded in to Lockheed. Sold to Mansdorf, then to ASI. Stored at Mojave, then flown to Santa Barbara. Used in B377MG Mini-Guppy conversion

LINE NUMBER: 15948   **MODEL 377-10-30**
Roll-out: 4 March 1949   **First flight:** 28 March 1949   **Delivered:** 22 June 1949
N74602: Northwest Airlines, *Stratocruiser Minneapolis- St Paul*, later *Stratocruiser Seattle-Tacoma*. Retired and traded in to Lockheed. Sold to Mansdorf, then to ASI, 1963. Stored at Mojave, then broken up

LINE NUMBER: 15949   **MODEL 377-10-30**
Roll-out: 18 March 1949   **First flight:** 9 April 1949   **Delivered:** 10 July 1949
N74603: Northwest Airlines, *Stratocruiser Chicago*, later *Stratocruiser New York*, *Stratocruiser Seattle-Tacoma*. Retired and traded in to Lockeed. Sold to Mansdorf, then to ASI, 1963. Stored, later broken up

LINE NUMBER: 15950   **MODEL 377-10-30**
Roll-out: 20 April 1949   **First flight:** 20 July 1949   **Delivered:** 11 August 1949
N74604: Northwest Airlines, *Stratocruiser New York*, later *Stratocruiser Detroit*. Retired and traded in to Lockheed. Sold to Mansdorf, then to ASI, 1963. Stored, later broken up

LINE NUMBER: 15951   **MODEL 377-10-30**
Roll-out: 6 May 1949   **First flight:** 10 August 1949   **Delivered:** 28 August 1949
N74605: Northwest Airlines, *Stratocruiser Chicago*, later *Stratocruiser Newark*. Retired and traded in to Lockheed. Sold to Mansdorf, then to ASI, 1963. Stored, later broken up

LINE NUMBER: 15952   **MODEL 377-10-30**
Roll-out: 15 June 1949   **First flight:** 22 August 1949   **Delivered:** 13 September 1949
N74606: Northwest Airlines, *Stratocruiser Chicago*, later *Stratocruiser Newark*. Retired and traded in to Lockheed. Sold to Mansdorf, then to ASI, 1963. Stored, later broken up

ABOVE: N76403 *Stratocruiser New York* (previously *Chicago*) was the third Model 377-10-30 delivered to Northwest Airlines. *via Walter Klein*

LINE NUMBER: 15953   **MODEL 377-10-30**
Roll-out: 9 August 1949   **First flight:** 11 September 1949   **Delivered:** 21 September 1949
N74607: Northwest Airlines, *Stratocruiser Honolulu*, later *Stratocruiser Rudolph* (with the radar nose). Damaged by exploding oxygen bottle, 15 June 1957. Not returned to service, sold on to RANSA. Scrapped for spares, Miami, February 1968

LINE NUMBER: 15954   **MODEL 377-10-30**
Roll-out: 28 September 1949   **First flight:** 10 October 1949   **Delivered:** 21 October 1949
N74608: Northwest Airlines, *Stratocruiser Tokyo*. Ditched into Puget Sound, 2 April 1956

LINE NUMBER: 15955   **MODEL 377-10-30**
Roll-out: 10 October 1949   **First flight:** 5 November 1949   **Delivered:** 18 November 1949
N74609: Northwest Airlines, *Stratocruiser Alaska*, later *Stratocruiser Portland*. Retired and traded in to Lockheed. Sold to Mansdorf, then to ASI, 1963. Stored, later broken up

LINE NUMBER: 15956   **MODEL 377-10-30**
Roll-out: 18 November 1949   **First flight:** 8 December 1949   **Delivered:** 21 December 1949
N74610: Northwest Airlines, *Stratocruiser Orient Express*, later *Stratocruiser Formosa*, *Stratocruiser Shanghai*. Retired and traded in to Lockheed. Sold to Mansdorf, then to ASI, 1963. Stored, later broken up

LINE NUMBER: 15957   **MODEL 377-10-29**
Roll-out: 23 February 1949   **First flight:** 12 March 1949   **Delivered:** 13 June 1949
N90941: American Overseas Airlines, *Flagship Great Britain*, later *Flagship Europe*, *Flagship Scandinavia*. To Pan American in September 1950, renamed *Clipper America*, later *Clipper Australia*. Crashed at Tokyo 9 July 1957

LINE NUMBER: 15958   **MODEL 377-10-29**
Roll-out: 3 June 1949   **First flight:** 8 July 1949   **Delivered:** 30 July 1949
N90942: American Overseas Airlines, *Flagship Europe*, later *Flagship Great Britain*. To Pan American in September 1950, renamed *Clipper Glory of the Skies*. Withdrawn 1960, stored Miami then sold to Mansdorf. To Aero Spacelines. Broken up, Mojave

Line Number: 15959   **Model 377-10-29**
Roll-out: 1 July 1949   **First flight:** 2 August 1949   **Delivered:** 20 August 1949
N90943: American Overseas Airlines, *Flagship Holland*, later *Flagship Europe*. To Pan American in September 1950, renamed *Clipper Sovereign of the Skies*. Crashed, mid-Pacific, 16 October 1956

Line Number: 15960   **Model 377-10-29**
Roll-out: 3 June 1949   **First flight:** 8 July 1949   **Delivered:** 30 July 1949
N90944: American Overseas Airlines, *Flagship Ireland*. To Pan American in September 1950, renamed *Clipper Romance of the Skies*. Crashed in the Pacific, en route to Hawaii, 9 November 1957

Line Number: 15961   **Model 377-10-29**
Roll-out: 15 September 1949   **First flight:** 23 September 1949   **Delivered:** 6 October 1949
N90945: American Overseas Airlines, *Flagship Norway*. To Pan American in September 1950, renamed *Clipper Monarch of the Skies*. Withdrawn 1960, stored Miami, then sold to Mansdorf. To RANSA, then repossessed by Boeing 1964 and registered to Miami Air Charters, 1967. Scrapped, Miami, April 1968. Parts to IAI

Line Number: 15962   **Model 377-10-29**
Roll-out: 20 October 1949   **First flight:** 29 October 1949   **Delivered:** 10 November 1949
N90946: American Overseas Airlines, *Flagship Sweden*. To Pan American in September 1950, renamed *Clipper Queen of the Skies*. Withdrawn 1961, stored San Francisco, then sold to IAI.
4X-AOG: Israeli Aircraft Industries, 2 February 1962
4X-FOD: re-registered for delivery flight, 24 March 1962. Converted to freighter, with rear clamshell doors and side cargo doors. Delivered to IDF/AF
4X-FPZ/096: delivered to Israel Defence Force/Air Force *Yodfat*, 1 February 1964. Struck off 1 October 1973

Above: G-ANUC *Clio*, was another ex-UAL Stratocruiser that joined BOAC. It was one of the aircraft loaned to Ghana Airways for its start-up services. *via APL*

LINE NUMBER: 15963   **MODEL 377-10-29**
Roll-out: 23 October 1949   **First flight:** 1 November 1949   **Delivered:** 18 November 1949
N90947: American Overseas Airlines, *Flagship Denmark*. To Pan American in September 1950, renamed *Clipper Good Hope*, later *Clipper Queen of the Pacific*. Withdrawn 1960, stored San Francisco, then sold to IAI.
4X-AOD: Israeli Aircraft Industries, 2 February 1962
4X-FOG: re-registered for delivery flight, 25 March 1962. Converted to freighter, with rear clamshell doors and side cargo doors. Delivered to IDF/AF
4X-FPX/098: delivered to Israel Defence Force/Air Force *Zipori*, 1 February 1964. Struck off 1 September 1975

LINE NUMBER: 15964   **MODEL 377-10-29**
Roll-out: 23 November 1949   **First flight:** 7 December 1949   **Delivered:** 5 January 1950
N90948: American Overseas Airlines, *Flagship Scotland*. To Pan American in September 1950, renamed *Clipper Eclipse*, later *Clipper Mandarin*. Withdrawn 1961, stored San Francisco, then sold to IAI.
4X-AOI: Israeli Aircraft Industries, 2 February 1962
4X-FOI: re-registered for delivery flight, 5 May 1962. Converted to freighter, with rear clamshell doors and side cargo doors. Delivered to IDF/AF
4X-FPY/097: delivered to Israel Defence Force/Air Force *Massada*, 1 February 1964. Struck off 16 October 1975

LINE NUMBER: 15965   **MODEL 377-34**
Roll-out: 17 June 1949   **First flight:** 8 July 1949   **Delivered:** 28 September 1949
N31225: United Air Lines, *Mainliner Hawaii*. Sold to BOAC 29 December 1954
G-ANTX: BOAC, RMA *Cleopatra*, re-delivered after conversion by Lockheed Aircraft Services 1 May 1955. Sold via the Babb Co to TAL
N108Q: Transocean Air Lines, delivered 27 July 1959
N413Q: re-registered. Never entered service. Sold to Airline Equipment Inc., then to Mansdorf. Sold on to Aero Spacelines Inc. Scrapped, Mojave, 1964

ABOVE: G-ANTY *Coriolanus*, a Model 377-10-34 was formerly N31226 *Mainliner Kauai* with United Air Lines. *via Aviation Picture Library*

LINE NUMBER: 15966   **MODEL 377-34**
Roll-out: 4 October 1949   **First flight:** 12 October 1949   **Delivered:** 28 October 1949
N31226: United Air Lines, *Mainliner Kauai*. Sold to BOAC 27 October 1954
G-ANTY: BOAC, RMA *Coriolanus*, re-delivered after conversion by Lockheed Aircraft Services 15 June 1955. Ghana Airways, 1959.
Sold via the Babb Company to TAL
N107Q: Transocean Air Lines, delivered 25 July 1959
N412Q: re-registered. Never entered service. Sold to Airline Equipment Inc., then to Mansdorf. Sold on to Aero Spacelines Inc. Scrapped,
Mojave

LINE NUMBER: 15967   **MODEL 377-34**
Roll-out: 7 November 1949   **First flight:** 21 November 1949   **Delivered:** 15 December 1949
N31227: United Air Lines, *Mainliner Hana Maui*. Sold to BOAC 16 December 1954
G-ANTZ: BOAC, RMA *Cordelia*, re-delivered after conversion by Lockheed Aircraft Services 23 June 1955. Ghana Airways, 1958, then
Nigerian Airways titles. Sold via the Babb Company to TAL
N106Q: Transocean Air Lines, delivered 10 April 1959
N411Q: re-registered. Never entered service. Sold to Airline Equipment Inc., then to Mansdorf. Sold on to Aero Spacelines Inc. Used for
B377-MG Mini-Guppy conversion

LINE NUMBER: 15968   **MODEL 377-34**
Roll-out: 7 November 1949   **First flight:** 18 November 1949   **Delivered:** 3 December 1949
N31228: United Air Lines, *Mainliner Waipahu*. Sold to BOAC 29 December 1954
G-ANUA: BOAC, RMA *Cameronian*, re-delivered after conversion by Lockheed Aircraft Services 6 June 1955. Nigerian Airways titles
1959. Sold via the Babb Company to TAL
N109Q: Transocean Air Lines, delivered 1 August 1959
N414Q: re-registered. Never entered service. Sold to Airline Equipment Inc., then to Mansdorf. Sold on to Aero Spacelines Inc., then
scrapped, Mojave

Line Number: 15969 **Model 377-34**
Roll-out: 1 December 1949 **First flight:** 9 December 1949 **Delivered:** 30 December 1949
N31229: United Air Lines, *Mainliner Hilo*. Sold to BOAC 22 September 1954
G-ANUB: BOAC, RMA *Calypso*, re-delivered after conversion by Lockheed Aircraft Services 9 April 1955. Leased to West African Airways, 1957 then carried Ghana Airways titles 1959. Withdrawn and broken up 8 January 1960, Stansted

Line Number: 15970 **Model 377-34**
Roll-out: 6 December 1949 **First flight:** 30 December 1949 **Delivered:** 28 January 1950
N31230: United Air Lines, *Mainliner Oahu*. Crashed into San Francisco Bay, 12 September 1951

Line Number: 15971 **Model 377-34**
Roll-out: 14 December 1949 **First flight:** 30 December 1949 **Delivered:** 28 January 1949
N31231: United Air Lines, *Mainliner Kano*. Sold to BOAC 1 December 1954
G-ANUC: BOAC, RMA *Clio*, re-delivered after conversion by Lockheed Aircraft Services 15 May 1955. Carried Nigerian Airways titles 1958. Withdrawn and broken up 8 January 1960, Stansted

Line Number: 15974 **Model 377-10-32**
Roll-out: 2 August 1949 **First flight:** 1 September 1949 **Delivered:** 16 November 1949
G-AKGH: BOAC RMA *Caledonia*. Retired and sold via the Babb Company to TAL. Delivered 2 August 1958
N137A: Transocean Air Lines
N402Q: re-registered TAL. Sold to Airline Equipment Inc., then to Mansdorf. Sold on to Aero Spacelines Inc. 1963, later scrapped, Mojave

Line Number: 15975 **Model 377-10-32**
Roll-out: 2 August 1949 **First flight:** 1 September 1949 **Delivered:** 16 November 1949
G-AKGI: BOAC RMA *Caribou*. West African Airways titles, 1957. Retired and sold via the Babb Company to TAL. Handed over 6 January 1958
N100Q: Transocean Air Lines
N405Q: re-registered TAL. Sold to Airline Equipment Inc., then to Mansdorf. Sold on to Aero Spacelines Inc. 1963, later scrapped, Mojave

Below: Israel's 4X-FPY was used for a range of transport tasks. *via Lon Nordeen*

ABOVE: Passengers relax aboard one of United Air Lines 'Mainliner' Stratocruisers. *via Walter Klein*

LINE NUMBER: 15976   MODEL 377-10-32
Roll-out: 9 December 1949   **First flight:** 29 December 1949   **Delivered:** 7 February 1950
G-AKGJ: BOAC RMA *Cambria*. Retired and sold via the Babb Company to TAL. Delivered 17 January 1958
N102Q: Transocean Air Lines
N407Q: re-registered TAL. Did not enter service. Sold to Airline Equipment Inc., then to Mansdorf. Sold on to Aero Spacelines Inc. 1963. Used for B377-PG Pregnant Guppy conversion

LINE NUMBER: 15977   MODEL 377-10-32
Roll-out: 16 December 1949   **First flight:** 17 January 1950   **Delivered:** 17 February 1950
G-AKGK: BOAC RMA *Canopus*. Ghana Airways titles, 1958. Retired and sold via the Babb Company to TAL. Handed over 3 March 1959
N104Q: Transocean Air Lines
N409Q: re-registered TAL. Sold to Airline Equipment Inc., then to Mansdorf. Sold on to Aero Spacelines Inc. 1963, later scrapped, Mojave

LINE NUMBER: 15978   MODEL 377-10-32
Roll-out: 21 December 1949   **First flight:** 25 January 1950   **Delivered:** 9 March 1950
G-AKGL: BOAC RMA *Cabot*. Retired and sold via the Babb Company to TAL. Handed over 13 September 1959
N86Q: Transocean Air Lines
N404Q: re-registered TAL. Sold to Airline Equipment Inc., then to Mansdorf. Sold on to Aero Spacelines Inc. 1963, later scrapped, Mojave

LINE NUMBER: 15979   MODEL 377-10-32
Roll-out: 21 December 1949   **First flight:** 25 January 1950   **Delivered:** 9 March 1950
G-AKGM: BOAC RMA *Castor*. Retired and sold via the Babb Company to TAL. Handed over 10 March 1959
N105Q: Transocean Air Lines
N410Q: re-registered TAL. Sold to Airline Equipment Inc., then to Mansdorf. Sold on to Aero Spacelines Inc. 1963. Stored at Oakland and scrapped, 1968

ABOVE: BOAC's Stratocruiser G-AKGM, RMA *Castor*, awaits its passengers at Prestwick Airport. This aircraft was the very last Stratocruiser to be built. *via William Doyle*

9 CHRONOLOGY

20 June 1942
Boeing draws up the preliminary engineering summary of what will become the XC-97 Stratofreighter prototype.

31 June 1942
Chief engineer Al Kelsey begins work on the XC-97 prototype.

9 November 1944
The prototype XC-97 makes its maiden flight. Boeing announces plans to build a commercial airliner version, to be known as the Stratocruiser.

28 November 1945
Boeing releases the final specification for the Model 377. Pan American World Airways signs the launch order for 20 Model 377-10-26 Stratocruisers, becoming the first of just five customers to take delivery of new-build aircraft.

February 1946
SILA becomes the second Stratocruiser customer, with an order for six Model 377-10-28s. In the event these aircraft are not taken up and are transferred to BOAC.

March 1946
Northwest Airlines becomes the third customer for the Stratocruiser, ordering ten Model 377-10-30s.

1 April 1946
American Overseas Airlines becomes the fourth Stratocruiser customer, with an order for ten aircraft to serve on its transatlantic routes.

6 August 1946
United Air Lines becomes the fifth Stratocruiser customer with an order for seven Model 377-10-34s.

18 October 1946
BOAC becomes the sixth and last of the original Stratocruiser customers, with an order for six Model 377-10-32s. BOAC's fleet will later grow to become second only to Pan American's.

2 July 1947
The first Model 377 Stratocruiser (NX90700) is rolled out of the factory.

8 July 1947
The prototype Stratocruiser (NX90700) makes its maiden flight with Boeing test pilot John B. Fonsaero at the controls. While in the air, the aircraft averaged a speed of 260mph (418km/h)

and reached an altitude of 1,000ft (3,353m). Boeing's order book for the type stood at 55.

17 July 1947
The United States Post Office issues a new 25¢ stamp, depicting a Stratocruiser flying north over San Francisco's Golden Gate Bridge. San Francisco will later become the main stepping-off point for the Stratocruiser's transpacific airline services.

28 September 1947
The second Stratocruiser (N1023V) takes to the air.

11 November 1947
The first two Stratocruisers pass the 100 hours flight time milestone, during ongoing flight tests.

31 January 1948
William M. Allen, Boeing's president, presents the first Stratocruiser to Pan American World Airways, at a ceremony in Portland, Oregon.

23 April 1948
A strike at Boeing threatens to affect the certification programme, so the three development aircraft are dispatched to Wichita, Kansas, to continue their flight trials.

12 December 1948
Pan American Airways announces that it is planning to acquire the assets of American Overseas Airlines.

31 January 1949
The first Boeing Model 377 Stratocruiser (N1025V) is formally handed over to launch customer Pan American Airways. The aircraft is flown from Boeing Field to Columbia Airport, Portland, Oregon, for the hand-over ceremony.

5 March 1949
In a ceremony at Washington DC, Pan American's first Stratocruiser is officially christened *Clipper America*, by Miss Margaret Truman, daughter of President Truman.

RIGHT: Father and daughter gaze up at the tail section of a brand-new Stratocruiser, towering above their heads. In terms of size alone the Stratocruiser had a revolutionary impact on the airline scene. The level of comfort it offered to passengers was a direct reflection of just how much available internal volume the aircraft had. *via Aviation Picture Library*

1 April 1949
Pan American puts the Stratocruiser into service, operating its first flight on the San Francisco–Honolulu route.

3 April 1949
The Pan American Stratocruiser *Clipper Flying Cloud* (N1028V) makes its first transatlantic proving flight, from New York to London. It is not yet ten years since the first Boeing Model 314 flying boat, *Yankee Clipper*, inaugurated regular commercial transatlantic air travel. The first Stratocruiser stops at Shannon Airport, in Ireland, and arrives in London on 4 April. She carries a crew of 17 and 42 passengers.

15 April 1949
The first scheduled Stratocruiser services on the North Atlantic begins when Pan American launches flights from New York to Bermuda.

2 June 1949
Pan American launches its three-times-a-week scheduled service from New York, Idlewild, to London.

10 June 1949
Pan American launches the first overnight all-sleeper service to London.

13 June 1949
American Overseas Airlines takes delivery of its first Stratocruiser, N90941 *Flagship Great Britain*.

19 June 1949
Boeing announces plans for the 99- to 103-seat Stratocoach. This developed, higher-capacity version is never built.

22 June 1949
The first Stratocruiser is delivered to Northwest Airlines.

1 July 1949
The first Stratocruiser for BOAC is rolled out at Renton. It will be delivered on 12 October.

7 July 1949
Technical troubles surface in the Stratocruiser when an aircraft is forced to turn back in flight for the first time. An idler gear in an engine oil pump failed over the Pacific and the aircraft returns safely. Boeing fits stronger idler gear shafts and bypass valves in all aircraft as a result.

10 August 1949
Pan American announces that it has carried a total of 3,393 passengers over the course of 72 transatlantic flights.

16 August 1949
Pan American launches daily service from the US to the UK, via Gander, in Newfoundland.

17 August 1949
American Overseas Airlines inaugurates its thrice-weekly services from the US to the UK. By 25 September services have risen to four per week.

1 September 1949
Northwest Airlines launches its Stratocruiser services, on the Seattle–Anchorage route.

21 September 1949
The 28th aircraft is delivered to Northwest Airlines. After only nine months Boeing has reached what will become the halfway point in Stratocruiser deliveries.

23 September 1949
Pan American operates its first transpacific proving flight between San Francisco–Honolulu–Tokyo.

12 October 1949
BOAC takes delivery of its first Stratocruiser, G-ALSA *Cathay*, in a ceremony at Seattle. The aircraft is ferried to London and arrives at Heathrow on 15 October. The direct flight from New York to London takes ten hours and 15 minutes.

17 October 1949
Pan American launches full scheduled service from San Francisco to Tokyo, via Honolulu.

5 November 1949
Pan American launched its New York–Shannon–Brussels–Frankfurt service.

6 December 1949
BOAC launches its first scheduled Stratocruiser service, on the London–Prestwick–New York route. For the first time Stratocruiser G-ALSA *Cathay* leaves Heathrow, bound for Idlewild.

12 December 1949
Pan American marks six months of transatlantic operations with the announcement that it has carried 12,000 passengers, and one third of those have flown by Stratocruiser.

17 December 1949
Pan American's *Clipper America* (N1025V) flies the first service to Auckland, New Zealand.

30 December 1949
Pan American receives the last of the 20 Stratocruisers that it ordered from Boeing. The airline is by far the largest Stratocruiser operator.

RIGHT: The C-97/KC-97 had a similar shape to the Stratocruiser, but a very different job. Fortune smiled on the military Model 367s, guaranteeing them an impressive production run and a lengthy service career. Sadly, the same could not be said of the Stratocruiser. *via Walter Klein*

ABOVE: This quartet of BOAC Stratocruisers is arranged around the airline's maintenance base at Heathrow. The aircraft in the foreground, G-AKGH *Caledonia*, was the first of BOAC's Model 377-10-32s, while G-ANTY *Coriolanus*, was one of the aircraft acquired from United in 1955. *via Aviation Picture Library*

ABOVE RIGHT: Newsmen gather round the Stratocruiser *Canopus* as HRH Queen Elizabeth II and the Duke of Edinburgh wave goodbye before setting off on their royal visit to Canada, in November 1953. *via Aviation Picture Library*

3 January 1950
Pan American Airlines officially changes its name to Pan American World Airways.

7 January 1950
In a ceremony at Prestwick, BOAC's Stratocruiser G-AKGH is officially named *Caledonia*, by the Minister of Civil Aviation, Lord Pakenham, and the Chairman of BOAC, Sir Miles Thomas. This is the first of BOAC's 'own' Model 377-10-32s to be delivered.

15 January 1950
United Air Lines launches Stratocruiser services.

1 May 1950
Pan American World Airways launches Stratocruiser services to Australia, with the first flight from San Francisco, via Honolulu to Sydney. The route will be shared with Douglas DC-4s until March 1951.

26 May 1950
Eight-tons of flood relief supplies, carried by BOAC's G-AKGH *Caledonia* from Heathrow to Winnipeg, becomes the largest single load ever to be flown across the Atlantic.

1 June 1950
Northwest Airlines launches domestic transcontinental services with its Stratocruisers.

4 July 1950
Pan American World Airways inaugurates its 'El Presidente' services to South America and Eva Peron christens the *Clipper Friendship* to mark the occasion. The journey from New York to Buenos Aires takes 26 hours and ten minutes.

25 September 1950
Pan American World Airways takes control of American Overseas Airlines and merges the two airline's Stratocruiser fleets. Pan American now operates 28 Stratocruisers.

24 October 1950
Having completed all its designated test flying tasks, the prototype Stratocruiser is redelivered to Pan American World Airways, to enter service as N1022V *Clipper Nightingale*. It becomes the company's 29th, and final, Stratocruiser.

17 December 1950
Pan American World Airways launches its New York–Paris sleeper service.

2 January 1951
Pan American World Airways extends its New York–Paris service to Rome. The Paris route is soon flown as a daily service, with aircraft continuing on to Rome three times a week.

7 March 1951
Pan American World Airways Stratocruisers take over the San Francisco–Honolulu–Sydney route full-time. They had shared it with DC-4s since operations began in May 1950.

7 October 1951
BOAC Stratocruiser G-AKGK *Canopus* carries HRH the Princess Elizabeth and the Duke of Edinburgh on a royal visit

to Canada. The flight routes via Gander and arrives in Dorval on 8 October.

12 September 1951
The first Stratocruiser is lost when United Airline's N31230 crashes during a training flight in San Francisco. All three crew onboard are killed.

29 April 1952
The first Stratocruiser on a scheduled passenger-carrying flight is lost when Pan American's N1039V crashes in Brazil. All 41 passengers and nine crew are killed.

7 September 1953
Pan American World Airways announces that in the first week of this month its Stratocruisers had carried 4,106 passengers across the Atlantic, more than the oceanliners *United States* and *Queen Elizabeth* combined.

7 May 1954
BOAC launches transatlantic services from Manchester, using a London–Manchester–Prestwick–New York routing.

4 September 1954
BOAC extends its 'Monarch' Stratocruiser flights to Frankfurt and Cairo, but the service is dropped in January 1955 due to a shortage of aircraft.

2 January 1955
United Air Lines operates its last Stratocruiser flight, and its aircraft are sold to BOAC — after just under five years of regular service.

1 April 1956
Boeing announces that the Stratocruiser fleet has flown 205,328,000nm over the course of 818,000 flying hours. The type has made 18,400 transatlantic crossings and 15,500 over the Pacific. Over 4,180,000 passengers have been carried.

10 May 1956
A Pan American World Airways aircraft, operated by the airline's Pacific Alaska division, becomes the first Stratocruiser to pass the five million-mile mark during a Pacific crossing somewhere between Wake Island and Guam.

1 July 1956
Pan American World Airways Stratocruisers launch their first scheduled service to Alaska.

3 May 1957
Wearing West African Airways titles, BOAC Stratocruiser G-AKGI launches Accra–Kano–Lagos services on behalf of WAA.

15 April 1958
Boeing contracts the Babb Company of New York to handle the sales of Stratocruisers traded back in exchange for the new Model 707 jets.

5 July 1958
BOAC begins to withdraw its Stratocruisers from service and the first aircraft for Transocean Air Lines is ferried to the USA.

16 July 1958
Using BOAC Stratocruiser, G-ANTZ, Ghana Airways launches services from Accra–Heathrow.

26 October 1958
Pan American World Airways replaces its Stratocruisers with the Boeing 707 on the New York –Paris route.

13 November 1958
RMA *Centaurus* flies the last scheduled BOAC Stratocruiser service from London–New York.

31 May 1959

BOAC flies its last ever scheduled Stratocruiser service, on the Accra–Kano–Barcelona–Heathrow route.

31 August 1959

G-ANUB flies the last service for Ghana Airways from Accra to Heathrow, bringing to an end all Stratocruiser operations by BOAC.

19 June 1960

Pan American World Airways drops scheduled flights to and from Alaska as the run-down of its Stratocruiser services finally begins.

11 July 1960

Transocean Air Lines suspends all operations and declares itself bankrupt. TAL was the last passenger airline to operate the Stratocruiser.

1 September 1960

From this date onwards Pan American World Airways Stratocruisers are limited to just two weekly services: Honolulu–Manila, and Saigon–Singapore.

ABOVE LEFT: Beauty and the beast — a Pan American Stratocruiser and a small but perfectly formed Ercoupe meet head-to-head. *John Stroud Collection/Aviation Picture Library*

15 September 1960

Northwest Airlines flies its last Stratocruiser service from New York to Minneapolis.

18 December 1960

Pan American World Airways aircraft N90947 makes the airline's last revenue-earning Stratocruiser flight, from Honolulu to San Francisco. This is the same route which, 12 years previously, saw the very first commercial Stratocruiser flights.

25 April 1962

Israel starts to take delivery of five Stratocruisers which will be modified to serve as specialist military transports.

6 September 1966

In Venezuela, RANSA declares bankruptcy and its active fleet of three Stratocruisers is withdrawn from service. RANSA was the last civil Stratocruiser operator in the world.

1 December 1975

The Israel Defence Force Air Force retires the last active Stratocruisers anywhere in the world.

BELOW: The sun has not quite set on the Stratocruiser story yet, if one includes the sole Super Guppy still in service with NASA. *via Kenneth Gibson*

INDEX